Lernkrimi Englisch

Das Skyline-Syndikat

Marlena Corcoran

Compact Verlag

Bisher sind in dieser Reihe erschienen:

- Compact Lernkrimi Englisch Grammatik
- Compact Lernkrimi Englisch Konversation
- Compact Lernkrimi Englisch GB/US Grammatik
- Compact Lernkrimi Englisch GB/US Konversation
- Compact Lernkrimi Englisch Grundwortschatz
- Compact Lernkrimi Englisch Aufbauwortschatz
- Compact Lernkrimi Französisch Grammatik
- Compact Lernkrimi Französisch Grundwortschatz
- Compact Lernkrimi Italienisch Grammatik
- Compact Lernkrimi Italienisch Grundwortschatz
- Compact Lernkrimi Spanisch Grammatik
- Compact Lernkrimi Spanisch Grundwortschatz

In der Reihe Lernthriller sind erschienen:

- Compact Lernthriller Englisch Grammatik
- Compact Lernthriller Englisch Konversation
- Compact Lernthriller Englisch Grundwortschatz
- Compact Lernthriller Englisch Aufbauwortschatz

In der Reihe English Mystery sind erschienen:

- Compact English Mystery Grundwortschatz
- Compact English Mystery Aufbauwortschatz

Weitere Titel sind in Vorbereitung.

Chefredaktion: Evelyn Boos
Redaktion: Sabine Framing
Fachredaktion: Todd Michael Rives
Produktion: Wolfram Friedrich
Titelillustration: Karl Knospe
Typographischer Entwurf: Maria Seidel
Umschlaggestaltung: Carsten Abelbeck

ISBN 3-8174-7573-X
7275731

Besuchen Sie uns im Internet: www.compactverlag.de

Vorwort

Mit dem neuen, spannenden Compact Lernkrimi können Sie Ihre Kenntnisse des britischen und des amerikanischen Englisch auf schnelle und einfache Weise vertiefen, auffrischen und überprüfen. Inspector Hudson erleichtert das Sprachtraining mit Action und Humor. Er und seine spannenden Kriminalfälle stehen im Mittelpunkt einer zusammenhängenden Story. Da Hudsons Fall ihn dieses Mal in die USA führt, greift die Story den Unterschied zwischen britischem und amerikanischem Englisch auf. Erläuterungen zur Kennzeichnung der sprachlichen Unterscheidungen finden Sie in den Benutzerhinweisen.

Der Krimi wird auf jeder Seite durch abwechslungsreiche und kurzweilige Übungen ergänzt, die das Lernen unterhaltsam und spannend machen.

Prüfen Sie Ihr Englisch in Lückentexten, Zuordnungs- und Übersetzungsaufgaben, in Buchstabenspielen und Kreuzworträtseln und lernen Sie, britisches und amerikanisches Englisch zu unterscheiden!

Ob im Bus oder in der Bahn, im Wartezimmer, zu Hause oder in der Mittagspause – das Sprachtraining im handlichen Format bietet die ideale Trainingsmöglichkeit für zwischendurch.

Schreiben Sie die Lösungen einfach ins Buch!

Die richtigen Antworten sind in einem eigenen Lösungsteil zusammengefasst.

Und nun kann die Spannung beginnen ...

Viel Spaß und Erfolg!

Die Ereignisse und die handelnden Personen in diesem Buch sind frei erfunden. Etwaige Ähnlichkeiten mit tatsächlichen Ereignissen oder lebenden Personen wären rein zufällig und unbeabsichtigt.

Inhalt

Benutzerhinweise 5
U-Bahn-Netz New York 6
Lernkrimi 7
Abschlusstest 127
Lösungen 136

Story

James Hudson arbeitet als Inspector bei der legendären Polizeibehörde Scotland Yard. Er ist einer der fähigsten Männer und wird immer dann zu Rate gezogen, wenn seine Kollegen mal wieder vor einem Rätsel stehen. Seine resolute und krimibegeisterte Haushälterin Miss Paddington unterstützt ihn stets mit liebevoller Fürsorge. Dieses Mal kann sie allerdings Hudsons Ermittlungen nicht mitverfolgen – sie darf lediglich seine Koffer packen ... Sein Fall führt ihn nämlich in die USA!

In New York ist die Zweigstelle der englischen Transatlantic Bank überfallen worden. Gerade der heimatverbundene Hudson soll nun die internationale Zusammenarbeit zwischen FBI und Scotland Yard initiieren. Mit seiner amerikanischen Kollegin Looey Looey durchkämmt er die Metropole. Das gefürchtete Skyline-Syndikat scheint mit dem Raubüberfall zu tun zu haben. Mysteriöse Leichenfunde deuten darauf hin, dass innerhalb des Syndikats heftige Machtkämpfe toben.

Durch geschicktes Kombinieren gelingt es den Ermittlern, die Schlinge um die Täter immer enger zu ziehen. Als ein zweiter Banküberfall passiert, kann schließlich das FBI dank Hudsons außergewöhnlicher Auffassungsgabe und dem entscheidenden Tipp eines Informanten schnell zuschlagen. Die Identifizierung der Täter überrascht sowohl das FBI als auch Scotland Yard ...

Benutzerhinweise

Der Text ist grundsätzlich in britischem Englisch verfasst. Amerikanische Ausdrücke sind zusätzlich nach folgendem Prinzip kursiv gekennzeichnet: Gibt es amerikanische Entsprechungen für die verwendeten britischen Wörter, stehen diese bei der ersten Verwendung des Wortes nach den britischen Wörtern in Klammern kursiv. Bei der weiteren Verwendung der Wörter entfällt dieser Zusatz.

Für Dialoge und direkte Rede gilt: Spricht ein Brite, wird die oben erklärte Kennzeichnung verwendet. Handelt es sich um einen amerikanischen Sprecher, verwendet dieser die amerikanischen Ausdrücke, die kursiv gesetzt sind. Die britische Entsprechung eines amerikanischen Ausdrucks steht bei der erstmaligen Nennung des Wortes in Klammern hinter dem kursiven amerikanischen Wort. Ab der zweiten Nennung des Wortes steht nur noch der kursive amerikanische Ausdruck.

Steht nach einem britischen oder amerikanischen Ausdruck eine Übersetzung in Doppelklammern heißt dies, dass der so gekennzeichnete Ausdruck in beiden Sprachräumen verwendbar ist. Sagt ein Brite zum Beispiel *dear* im Sinne von „teuer", würde ein Amerikaner *expensive* sagen. *Expensive* kann man aber auch im britischen Englisch sagen – das Wort steht also kursiv in Doppelklammern hinter dem Wort *dear.*

Grundsätzlich wird bei der Einordnung von Wörtern als britisch bzw. amerikanisch die Auswahl nach der Häufigkeit der Verwendung des Wortes im jeweiligen Sprachraum bzw. nach der Herkunft des Wortes getroffen. Wird also zum Beispiel das Wort *sneakers* als amerikanischer Ausdruck gekennzeichnet, so heißt dies, dass das Wort im Amerikanischen häufiger verwendet wird bzw. dass es wie in diesem Fall ursprünglich aus dem Amerikanischen stammt und inzwischen manchmal auch im Britischen verwendet wird.

The New York City Subway System

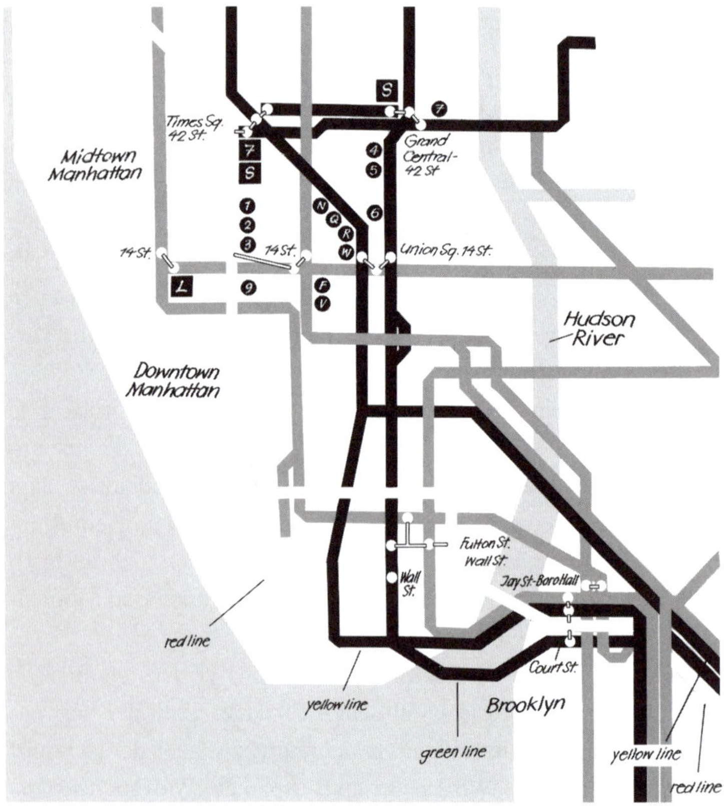

Skyline Syndicate

Inspector James Hudson woke up to the sound of birds singing outside his bedroom window. "What a lovely day!" he thought. "It's rare enough that the sun shines in London, and today is my day off!"

Hudson was one of the best detectives at Scotland Yard. He had solved many important cases, including disappearing artwork and a shocking mummy theft.

Sir Reginald, Hudson's superior *(boss)* at Scotland Yard, had told Hudson that after all his hard work, it was high time for him to take a holiday *(vacation)*.

Übung 1: Kreuzen Sie die richtige Antwort an!

1. What time is it, please?
a) ☐ It is nine o'clock mornings.
b) ☒ It is almost nine o'clock.

2. What's the weather like today?
a) ☒ It's sunny today.
b) ☐ It's sunning today.

3. Do you have to go to work today?
a) ☐ Yes, I have work today.
b) ☒ Yes, I must go to work today.

4. What kind of work does he do?
a) ☐ He is detective at Scotland Yard.
b) ☒ He is a detective at Scotland Yard.

5. Did your supervisor tell you?
a) ☒ Yes, my supervisor told me.
b) ☐ Yes, my supervisor told to me.

6. Are you going on holiday?
a) ☐ Yes, I go on holiday.
b) ☒ Yes, I am going on holiday.

7. Do you go on holiday every summer?
a) ☐ No, I go on the holiday later in the year.
b) ☒ No, I go on holiday later in the year.

"Very well, sir," said Hudson. "But just one day. I don't really care to ((like to)) go away. I'm a city man, and London is the place I love the best. Perhaps I'll spend the day at the British Museum."

"Why don't you take a week, Hudson? You could travel to somewhere exotic: fresh sights, interesting food, a different language …" said Sir Reginald. "You could book one of those package tours to someplace sunny and warm. Why not Egypt? You could pay a visit to that mummy that was returned to his resting place, thanks to the way you solved that last crime!"

"Oh, no, sir," replied Hudson. "Thank you very much, but that's not for me. I've never left the United Kingdom."

"What, never?" asked Sir Reginald. "Not even for a jaunt to, say, New York? I hear those Rockettes speak our language!"

Inspector Hudson looked shocked.

"Chorus girls are not my cup of tea, sir ((I'm not interested in chorus girls, sir))," said Hudson politely.

"You're a queer bird *(You're a strange guy)*," said Sir Reginald. "But you're a fine detective. Spend your day off in London, if you like. But do get some rest *(But be sure to get some rest)*!"

Übung 2: Formulieren Sie die Sätze zu Fragen um!

1. Inspector Hudson hasn't been to New York.

____

2. The Rockettes are chorus girls.

____

3. They are dancers in New York.

____

4. Inspector Hudson is shocked.

____

5. Inspector Hudson isn't interested in chorus girls.

____

6. He will spend his day off at the British Museum.

____

7. Sir Reginald thinks he is a queer bird.

____

So it was that, after a good night's sleep, James Hudson was ready for a proper English breakfast and a day in town.
Hudson heard the teakettle whistle and knew that his faithful housekeeper, Miss Paddington, would be setting out a soft-boiled egg with toast and the bitter orange marmalade he liked so much.

Übung 3: Ordnen Sie die Buchstaben zu einem sinnvollen Wort!

Hudson detected a delicious (1. mlles) smell ________ in the air.

Why, Miss Paddington is frying rashers ((2. coban bacon ________))!

Speckscheibe

How (3. gnlo) long had it been since he took the (4. etmi) time to sit (5. ownd) down to rashers and (6. gegs) eggs? He was always in (7. chus) such a hurry to get to (8. krow) work at Scotland Yard.

Hudson was dressed in a wink. Out of habit, he reached for his detective's badge.

"Not today, old man ((my friend))," he thought. He put it back on his chest of drawers *(dresser)* and went in to breakfast.

"Good morning, sir," said Miss Paddington. "It's so good to see you looking relaxed on your day off."

"Breakfast looks delicious," said Hudson. He reached for the tea and filled his cup.

"It's a good English breakfast," smiled his housekeeper.

ÜBUNG 4 !

Übung 4: Was isst Inspector Hudson an Werktagen zum Frühstück? Setzen Sie das richtige Wort ein, um das Rätsel zu lösen!

1. What kind of marmalade does he prefer?

bitter orange

2. How is his egg cooked?

soft-boiled

3. What does Inspector Hudson drink with his breakfast?

tea

4. What is his special treat this morning?

r a [s] h e r s

5. What does he also spread on his bread?

b u [t] t e r

Lösung: t o a s t

As he finished his rashers and eggs, Hudson thought, "I really must take the time to go over the household expenses. Everything has become so dear ((expensive))!"

Übung 5: Tragen Sie eine amerikanische Entsprechung für die folgenden britischen Wörter bzw. die folgenden britischen Wendungen ein!

ÜBUNG 5 !

1. holiday — vacation
2. rashers — bacon
3. not my cup of tea — I'm not interested
4. Do get some rest! — Get some rest
5. dear (costly) — expensive
6. superior — boss

He was sure that Miss Paddington was a very good housekeeper, and did her best to keep expenses low. She understood that even the very best detectives in Scotland Yard were not paid a great deal of money. Just last week she had asked him if he would like her to purchase a less expensive brand of marmalade for his breakfast.

"Miss Paddington," Hudson said. "Would you have a moment to go over the household expenses?"

"Certainly, sir," replied Miss Paddington. "I'll get my records."

Together, they went over the books. Miss Paddington had carefully written down the amounts of money that Hudson had given to her. She had also recorded every penny she had spent.

"Hmm," said Inspector Hudson. "I think I have solved this mystery. Here's where the money is disappearing!"

Hudson pointed to something on page three.

Übung 6: Welches Wort ist das „schwarze Schaf"? Unterstreichen Sie das nicht in die Reihe passende Wort!

1. money, penny, teakettle, expense, shilling
2. holiday, work, tour, travel, visit
3. sun, cloud, bird, rain, fog
4. museum, artwork, mummy, badge, painting
5. detective, supervisor, direction, housekeeper, singer
6. mystery, habit, theft, crime, robbery
7. say, agree, ask, book, inquire

"You don't believe, sir – " exclaimed Miss Paddington, as her face turned red. "I mean to say, you don't think that I … "

"Why, Miss Paddington! Why do you look so upset?" asked Hudson. "You don't think I stole the household money?"

"You!" exclaimed Inspector Hudson. "Of course not!"

"I did offer to purchase a less expensive marmalade, sir!" Miss Paddington cried.

“We may need to economise ((economize)) a bit,” agreed Hudson. “But I don’t think the problem is the marmalade. You don’t have to be a detective from Scotland Yard to see that the culprit is the Bentley.”

Angeklagte
Schuldige

Übung 7: Was sind die Missverständnisse in der Unterhaltung?

1. Inspector Hudson thinks that

a) [x] he has solved the financial mystery.

b) [ ] he has lost all his money.

2. Miss Paddington thinks that

a) [ ] she has made a mistake in arithmetic.

b) [x] she should buy less expensive marmalade.

3. Inspector Hudson believes that

a) [ ] his Bentley has been stolen.

b) [x] his Bentley is very expensive to maintain.

4. Miss Paddington believes that

a) [ ] Inspector Hudson spends too much money.

b) [x] Inspector Hudson thinks she stole his money.

Miss Paddington smiled. She knew that her employer had a weakness for his old but beautiful car. She was proud of her employer’s very British habits.
“It’s a beautiful car,” said Miss Paddington. “And it is so much

more elegant than driving a brand new automobile. You're not like those flashy Americans, Mr *(Mr.)* Hudson," she said. "I hear some of them buy a new car every year!"
Miss Paddington sighed.
"Though who can say," she said. "Perhaps it would be very nice."

ÜBUNG 8 !

Übung 8: Unterstreichen Sie das zutreffende Wort!

1. Inspector Hudson's car is old/new.
2. His Bentley is ugly/beautiful.
3. Inspector Hudson is modest/flashy.
4. Inspector Hudson is trendy/conservative.
5. He is very British/American.
6. Miss Paddington is a careless/careful housekeeper.
7. Sir Reginald is angry/glad that Hudson will take a day off.
8. Sir Reginald is surprised/disappointed that Hudson does not wish to go to Egypt.
9. Inspector Hudson enjoys/dislikes his breakfast.
10. Miss Paddington is ashamed/proud of her employer.

"What's this?" asked Inspector Hudson brightly.
"Are you turning American on me, after all these years?"
"Well," said Miss Paddington. "It would be something to see, just once, don't you think? A whole new world, with everything in it new!"
"You surprise me, Miss Paddington!" exclaimed Inspector Hudson.
"But wherever ((where)) do they get the money? I can hardly keep my household in marmalade! At this rate," said Miss Paddington, "I shall ((will)) have to rob a bank!"
Just then, the phone rang.

Übung 9: Worin besteht die Überraschung?

1. Sir Reginald was surprised that

a) ☒ Hudson is not interested in the Rockettes.

b) ☐ the mummy was back in Egypt.

2. Hudson was surprised that

a) ☐ package tours to Egypt are so dear.

b) ☒ Sir Reginald mentioned chorus girls.

3. Sir Reginald was surprised that

a) ☒ Hudson had never left the United Kingdom.

b) ☐ Hudson travelled *(traveled)* often to the United States.

4. Miss Paddington is surprised that

a) ☐ she has made a mistake in arithmetic.

b) ☒ her employer may think she has done something wrong.

5. Inspector Hudson is surprised that

a) ☒ Miss Paddington admires his Bentley.

b) ☒ Miss Paddington admires new things.

6. Miss Paddington is surprised that

a) ☒ Americans can afford new cars every year.

b) ☐ Americans can afford to spend their holidays in Europe.

7. Hudson and Miss Paddington are both surprised that

a) ☐ the teakettle boils.

b) ☒ the phone rings.

“It’s for you,” whispered Miss Paddington, as she handed the phone to her employer. “It’s Sir Reginald.”

“Hudson here.”

“The Transatlantic Bank has been robbed, Hudson! Pack your bags immediately!” barked Sir Reginald.

! ÜBUNG 10

Übung 10: Setzen Sie die passenden Wörter aus der folgenden Liste in die Lücken ein!

(shot, robbed, airport, million, asking, replied, instantly, bag, office)

“But Sir Reginald,” 1. replied ________ Hudson, puzzled. “It’s right in the City.”

“Not that Transatlantic Bank!” cried Sir Reginald. “The one in New York! Three men have 2. robbed ________ the midtown Manhattan branch of the Transatlantic Bank. They made off with well over a 3. million ________ dollars! A security guard was badly injured and a police constable *(police officer)* was 4. shot ________. The Federal Bureau of Investigation (FBI) called me just this instant, 5. asking ________ me to send them my best man.”

“But sir –” Hudson began.

“Never mind ‘sir’, Hudson! I want you in my 6. office ________ for a briefing 7. instantly ! The FBI believes this is the work of the Skyline Syndicate."

Sir Reginald paused for breath.

"Have your housekeeper pack your things, Hudson, and you can stop off at your flat *(apartment)* and pick up your 8. bag on your way to the 9. airport !

I'll explain everything when you get here – but hurry! Goodbye!"
"Goodbye, sir."
Within a quarter of an hour, Inspector Hudson was sitting in front of Sir Reginald's desk.

Übung 11: Unterstreichen Sie das passende Wort!

"Things are not looking 1. good/well in New York," began Sir Reginald. "The FBI is very 2. worryfull/worried. This morning's crime was not an amateur job. Most people think a bank robbery is as simple as walking into a bank with a gun and shouting 3. ordinarily/loudly, 'Give me the money!'"
"That's a fool's game," agreed Hudson 4. immediately/strangely. "There isn't that much cash to be had. Security is tight within a bank during normal business hours. Chances are that the thief will be caught 5. sudden/straightaway *(right away).*"
"The job in New York was very well 6. played/planned," continued Sir Reginald. "The robbers knew 7. exact/exactly when a large delivery of cash would be made to the cashpoint machines *(Automatic Teller Machines, ATM machines).* It was very 8. soon/

early in the morning, before the main part of the bank was open for business."

Hudson raised an eyebrow.
"Did they attack the security van while it was on the way to the bank?" Hudson asked. Hudson remembered that two of the men on Scotland Yard's Most Wanted List had robbed security vans on the roads outside of London.
"This was a very urban crime, Hudson. The robbers waited until the security van had parked in front of the bank. They attacked just as the security guard was bringing bags of money from the van to the cashpoint machines in the bank lobby."
"I see," said Hudson. "And on a busy day in midtown Manhattan, those machines might be stocked with – "
"A million and a half dollars."

ÜBUNG 12 !

Übung 12: Streichen Sie die Sätze durch, die inhaltlich nicht zum Text passen!

"And one wouldn't even need to get into the main area of the bank," observed Hudson. "~~My mother told me so.~~"
"Just as the door to the lobby was opened by the guard himself," continued Sir Reginald, "the robbers came up behind him and hit him in the head. ~~He gave them the bill. Dinner is getting cold!~~ The poor man was taken to Casualty *(the emergency room),* and is still in hospital *(in the hospital).*"
"Very terrible, indeed," said Hudson. "~~You have told me this before.~~ And what's this you said about a police constable being shot? ~~Why should I believe you?~~"
"It was around five o'clock in the morning," explained Sir Regi-

nald. "I offered him help. There was almost no one on the street. A young off-duty police constable happened to be coming home from a night on the town. He rushed to the aid of the guard – and was shot in the chest. He bought a new car. He is still in surgery."

"That is very terrible, indeed, sir. But what does this have to do with Scotland Yard?"
"You've heard of the new program in international law enforcement," said Sir Reginald. "The United Kingdom and the United States are cooperating to solve cases that involve both countries."
Hudson nodded.
"This case is a prime candidate for cooperation between law enforcement agencies in New York and London for two reasons," said Sir Reginald. "First, the Transatlantic Bank operates in both the United States and the United Kingdom. The robbery took place in New York, but the bank's main headquarters are in London."
"And the second reason," added Hudson, "is that this robbery may be the work of the Skyline Syndicate."
"Correct," said Sir Reginald. "The Skyline Syndicate is becoming larger, more powerful – and, we fear, international."

Übung 13: Korrigieren Sie die vorgegebenen Wörter!

"If indeed ((if in fact)) they got away with a million and a half dollars this morning, the Skyline Syndicate must soon begin a (1. majorish) ________________ money laundering operation," mused Hudson. "That will quickly involve them in (2. internationalising) ((internationalizing)) ________________ crime."

ÜBUNG 13 !

"Good point, Hudson. One must think in terms of a (3. worldly-wide) ________________ network of crime." The older man sighed. "The world has changed since the time I was a (4. youngling) ________________ detective. Oh, we still get the (5. oddity) ________________ crime of passion, or (6. freeforlance) ________________ burglar. And there are always (7. anti-individual) ________________ cases of severe sociopathy. But once there is a (8. hugely) ________________ sum of money to be made …"

Hudson completed Sir Reginald's thought. "These days, all crime is (9. internationally) ________________ crime."

"Exactly. That is why I am sending you to New York, to cooperate with the FBI."

Hudson looked quite (10. miserabel) ________________, but said nothing.

"Let's get back to this morning's crime," said Sir Reginald. "The robbers wore women's (11. nilon) ________________ stockings pulled over their heads."

"That's not terribly original, sir," said Hudson.

"It's not original," said Sir Reginald. "But it's frightfully *(extremely)* effective. No one could identify a man whose features are so (12. distworted) ________________." Sir Reginald sighed.

Übung 14: Welche Satzteile gehören zusammen? Ordnen Sie zu!

1. The FBI	2	wore nylon stockings.
2. The robbers	4	made tea and toast.
3. Hudson	5	got a phone call.
4. Miss Paddington	1	noted similarities.
5. Sir Reginald	7	may be going international.
6. Scotland Yard	3	says it is not original.
7. The Skyline Syndicate	6	will cooperate with the FBI.

"Within an hour, the FBI had posted a short clip of the robbery in progress on their internet site." Sir Reginald rubbed his eyes. "I fear I am getting too old for this. Do you remember back when Scotland Yard decided to put the Most Wanted List on the internet?"

"I recall the discussions pro and con, sir," said Hudson. "Some of us at the Yard felt that it was as good as posting an instructional manual on how to get away with murder, as it were."

"Quite right ((That's right)), Hudson," replied Sir Reginald. "And do you recall the heated arguments concerning the videos?"

"My goodness, yes," said Hudson. "Once it became possible to include a video clip along with a photograph of the fugitive, the question became whether indeed we should do so. You were dead set against putting video clips of crimes in progress on the internet."

Übung 15: Wie verwendet man das Wort ***video****? Tragen Sie entweder das Wort* ***richtig*** *in die Lücke ein oder verbessern Sie!*

1. Did you videotape the soccer game? ✓

2. Let's video (tape) the party! ____________

3. Do you have a videotape of the movie?

4. Let's put the video clips on the internet!

5. Did she buy a video camera?

6. Streaming video is very trendy.

7. Did you watch video last night?

8. What was your favourite *(favorite)* video?

9. Let's rent some video!

"It did seem a bit tasteless," said Sir Reginald. "It's terribly useful, of course, when a surveillance camera catches a criminal in the act. It's astonishing how often we now have an actual recording of a robbery in progress."

"It doesn't always guarantee that we catch the robber," said Hudson quietly, thinking of more than one video clip that had been on the internet for years.

"I must admit that I was wrong," said Sir Reginald.
"You don't say! *(Really?)*" Hudson almost smiled.
"A surveillance camera at the bank recorded this morning's crime," said Sir Reginald. "I have downloaded the video clip."
"Sir! I would never have guessed that you – "
"Never mind what you would have guessed, Hudson. Kindly restrict your guessing to your official duties!"
Hudson's eyes sparkled.
"As you wish, sir."
"You can copy this clip onto your laptop and study it on the aeroplane *(airplane)* to New York. I just wanted you to have a shufty *(take a look)* straightaway."

Übung 16: Tragen Sie jeweils eine passende höfliche Wendung in die Lücke ein!
(It seems to me that, It's not my cup of tea, Perhaps I misunderstood, It's possible, Might it be, May I, Could we possibly, I must admit that, Let me)

1. ______________________________ I was wrong.
2. ______________________________ we've settled this issue.
3. ______________________________ to see this differently
4. ______________________________ time to call it a day?
5. ______________________________ get that for you.
6. ______________________________, but please go right ahead.
7. ______________________________ your point.

8. ______________________________ meet a bit later?

9. ___________________________ have another piece of cake?

Sir Reginald clicked on the video file on the desktop of his computer and pointed to the screen.
"There's the main man, wearing that impossible nylon stocking over his head."
The first man to approach the guard was followed closely by two other men wearing the same disguise.
Hudson almost smiled again, but then he remembered that the masked robbers had viciously attacked the security guard and shot a police constable.

ÜBUNG 17

Übung 17: Bringen Sie die Sätze dieses Dialogs in die richtige zeitliche Reihenfolge!

1. What changed your mind?
2. I remember the discussion.
3. I heard the FBI found the videos useful.
4. Do you remember when the topic first came up?
5. What was your first reaction?
6. I think we should put the videos on the internet.
7. I thought the idea was tasteless.
8. What should we do now?

Lösung: _ _ _ _ _ _ _ _

"The video clip stops before the security guard is struck from behind with the butt of a pistol," said Sir Reginald. "They tell me it is a horrible sight. It is clear that these are hardened criminals. I want you to be very careful over there, Hudson. The robbers are armed and dangerous."

"Yes, sir."

"Your colleagues across the Atlantic will certainly have a lot to say about the fact that British police constables do not carry firearms," Sir Reginald said. "Criminals surely do."

"I'm not a criminal," said Inspector Hudson with a slight smile. "I'm just doing my job."

"And a very fine job you do of it, Hudson *(And you do a very good job, Hudson),*" said his superior. "That is why I am sending you to New York."

Übung 18: Formulieren Sie die Sätze in amerikanischem Englisch!

ÜBUNG 18 !

1. I shall ring you up tomorrow! ____________________

____

2. I left it in my flat! ____________________

____

3. Straightaway, sir! ____________________

4. Take her to Casualty! ____________________

____

5. You don't say! ____________________

6. Have a shufty! ____________________

7. Quite right! ____________________

The phone rang on Sir Reginald's desk.

"Good morning, Sir Reginald," said the caller. "Or should I say, 'Good afternoon'? This is Supervisory Special Agent O'Leary of the FBI. I'm calling with bad news."

Sir Reginald took out a handkerchief and wiped his face.

"The police *officer* who was shot during the robbery this morning is dead."

"I'm terribly sorry," said Sir Reginald.

Hudson looked up.

"The *officer* was shot in the chest," said Agent O'Leary. "He was in surgery for six hours, but the doctors couldn't save his life."

"And the security guard?" asked Sir Reginald.

"Hanging in there."

"I am sending you my very best detective," said Sir Reginald. "His name is Hudson; Inspector Hudson. He is booked on a flight that will get him into JFK at four o'clock local time."

"Ask him to report to my office as soon as he checks into his hotel," said Agent O'Leary. "And Sir Reginald?"

"Yes?"

"I assume he will be armed."

"Your request is duly noted," replied Sir Reginald.

"But we servants of Her Majesty simply do things a bit differently from you chaps *(men)*."

Sir Reginald rang off *(hung up the phone)*.

"Killing a police constable is an extremely serious offence. Are there any suspects?" asked Hudson.

"It was most definitely a professional job," said Sir Reginald. "That is clear not only from the amount of money involved, but also from the violence of the attack on the guard and the constable. That brings us back to the Skyline Syndicate."

Sir Reginald sighed.

Übung 19: Unterstreichen Sie jeweils die richtige Präposition!

“The problem is that the details 1. on/of the robbery don’t fit 2. to/with other crimes known to have been committed 3. by/for the Skyline Syndicate,” he said.
“The New York Police Department (NYPD), which is working together 4. with/against the FBI on this, believes that something strange is going on 5. in/over the Syndicate these days. It could even be that a relatively unknown member 6. by/of the Syndicate is rising to power.”

“Do they have any idea who it might be?”
“The main suspect is called – ” Sir Reginald tapped his desk and sighed.
“Yes?”
“Fat Frankie. He weighs twenty stone *(two hundred and eighty pounds)* and is a mean man with a baseball bat. He has never been convicted of a crime. However, he has twice been tried for attempted murder. In each case, he was declared not guilty of attacks that left two men with permanent head injuries.”
“Ghastly ((Awful)),” murmured Hudson.
“The other suspect is Salvatore del Monaco. He has already spent time in the state penitentiary for robbery of a more juvenile sort. He pulled a gun on a off-license clerk and demanded money. While the clerk was handing over the cash, Sal decided to ask for a bottle of whiskey as well. The clerk objected that Sal did not look old enough to purchase strong alcoholic drink *(liquor)*. Sal showed the clerk his identification, which the clerk memorised ((memorized)) and reported to the police.”
“I suppose we can be grateful that not every case requires advanced detective skills.”

ÜBUNG 20 !

Übung 20: Mit welchen Wörtern kann man diese Mitglieder des Skyline Syndicate beschreiben?
(mean, robber, not clever, baseball bat, overweight, gun, attempted murder, liquor store)

1. Fat Frankie

---

2. Salvatore del Monaco

"He may not be a genius, Hudson, but the man is dangerous. He knows he can be tricked, and so he would rather shoot than talk. I urge you in the strongest possible terms to keep your wits about you *(keep a sharp eye out)*!"
"I shall remain alert, sir," said Hudson. "I shall also keep an open mind. It's in many ways the hardest and the most important part of the job."
Sir Reginald handed Hudson a fresh stack of paper.
"This information about this morning's case arrived by fax. You can read it on the aeroplane."
Inspector Hudson leafed through the pages.
"But Sir Reginald," said Hudson. "I don't understand a word of American English."
He looked at the papers.
"'*License plate*' (number plate). What on earth does that mean? Or – good heavens – '*pantyhose*' (tights)?"
"I think that you've solved much stranger mysteries than American English, Hudson," said Sir Reginald. "Your plane leaves in two hours. Have a good journey *(trip)* and good luck, old boy."

Übung 21: Wie antwortet man kurz und höflich?

1. Your supervisor asks to speak to you immediately.

a) ☒ "Certainly, sir!"
b) ☐ "Certainly, mister!"

2. Your supervisor asks you to fetch a certain document.

a) ☐ "Right away, sir!"
b) ☒ "Right now, sir!"

3. Your supervisor instructs you to take a holiday.

a) ☒ "Very nice, sir!"
b) ☒ "Very well, sir."

4. Your supervisor tells you to finish a task today.

a) ☒ "As you wish, sir."
b) ☐ "As you imagine, sir!"

5. Your supervisor asks whether the post has arrived yet.

a) ☒ "Not yet, ma'am!"
b) ☐ "Not likely, ma'am!"
c) ☐ "Not really, ma'am!"

6. The waiter asks if everything is to your liking.

a) ☒ "Yes, thank you!"
b) ☐ "Yes, sir!"
c) ☐ "Yes, waiter."

7. The waiter asks if you would care for another drink.

a) ☐ "Not on your life!"
b) ☒ "No, thank you."

Inspector Hudson returned home to pick up his kit. His housekeeper, Miss Paddington, was fretting terribly ((was very upset)) because he was off to New York. She was rather fond of her employer.

"I hear it's completely uncivilised ((uncivilized))!" Miss Paddington cried. "This could be your most dangerous mission!"

Miss Paddington dropped the shirt she was folding. "And what if you must ring us immediately, and you don't have a – what is it called – *quarter* (coin worth twenty-five *cents*) for the, as they say, *phone booth* (phone box)?"

"I'll ring you on my mobile," said Inspector Hudson. "Now do hurry."

"You'll *call me on your cellphone,* as they say over there!" said Miss Paddington, archly.

ÜBUNG 22 !

Übung 22: Nennen Sie ein äquivalentes Wort in britischem Englisch!

1. *cellphone* mobile
2. *license plate* number plate
3. *vacation* holiday
4. *phone booth* phone box
5. ((fourteen pounds)) ____________
6. *airplane* aeroplane

"Wherever did you pick up these expressions?" asked Hudson.

"Well," smiled Miss Paddington, "I've always dreamed of going to New York."

For all his skill as a detective, Hudson had never guessed Miss Paddington's dream.

"Go on now," said Miss Paddington. "And do be careful. It's a big city. I hear the Underground *(subway)* can be dangerous, if you don't know your way around! Promise me you'll stay out of the Tube *(subway)*, and take a cab directly from the airport to your hotel."

Übung 23: Was würden Sie über Ihren Urlaub sagen?

1. How long will you be on holiday?
a) ☒ "I shall spend one week in Bath."
b) ☐ "I spend one week in Bath."

2. Where will you go on holiday?
a) ☐ "I shall fly in Paris."
b) ☒ "I shall fly to Paris."

3. Will you go abroad?
a) ☒ "I never leave the United Kingdom."
b) ☐ "I never leave out the United Kingdom."

4. Will you visit your family?
a) ☐ "I visit to my family every year."
b) ☒ "I visit my family every year."

5. Will you stay in the city?
a) ☐ "I plan to stay by London."
b) ☒ "I plan to stay in London."

6. Will you be home soon?
a) ☒ "I shall be home in a week."
b) ☐ "I shall be home after a week."

7. Will you go to Egypt?
a) ☒ "That's not for me."
b) ☐ "That's not about me."

It was a long flight from London to New York. Inspector James Hudson stepped out of the airline terminal at JKF Airport into the bright sunlight of an autumn afternoon.
"So this is New York," he thought.
Hudson remembered his promise to Miss Paddington. He must take a cab from the airport directly to his hotel. Inspector Hudson looked around for a big, black cab with room for his luggage.
Then he remembered that in New York, many cabs are yellow. He saw a yellow car go by and stop where some people had queued up *(lined up)*. There was a man in uniform at the head of the queue *(line)*.
"Taxi, sir?" asked the man in uniform. "The *line* starts at the *curb* (kerb) here. Where are you going?"
Inspector Hudson showed the man the address. The man wrote down a number on a card, and told Inspector Hudson to pay no more than this for the ride.
"Have a nice visit to New York," said the man.
A yellow cab pulled up, and Inspector Hudson got in.
"Where to, sir?" asked the driver.
"The Ivy Club," said Inspector Hudson. "Fifth Avenue and Forty-fourth Street, please."
"Nice address," said the driver, looking back at Inspector Hudson in the mirror. "Are you from Boston?"

“I’m from England,” replied Inspector Hudson. “But watch out!” he cried. “There’s an accident ahead!”

The cab driver looked ahead at two vehicles off to the side of the road.

“I don’t think that’s an accident,” said the driver. “They’re in the *breakdown lane* (near side lane). I think he’s just out of *gas* (petrol). That *truck* (lorry) pulled over to give him a hand. See, he’s getting a can of *gas* out of the *trunk* (boot).”

The cab driver explained, “There aren’t many *gas stations* (petrol stations) in the city, and it can be a long drive to the airport, even on the *highway* (motorway).”

Inspector Hudson tried to relax.

Übung 24: Nennen Sie ein äquivalentes Wort in amerikanischem Englisch!

1. near side lane ____________
2. petrol gas
3. motorway highway
4. boot ____________
5. petrol station gas station
6. lorry ____________
7. kerb ____________
8. queue ____________
9. Tube ____________

"I might have been born in England myself," said the driver. "My grandparents wanted to leave India, and had a hard time deciding whether to go to London or New York."
Inspector Hudson noted the driver's name, which was posted in the cab: Arjun Patel.
"Just think," said the driver. "I might be driving on the wrong side of the road!"

ÜBUNG 25 !

Übung 25: Wie nennt man die Einwohner der folgenden Orte und Länder?

1. London ____________________
2. England ____________________
3. New York ____________________
4. America ____________________
5. India ____________________
6. Italy ____________________
7. Brooklyn ____________________
8. Manhattan ____________________
9. New Jersey ____________________
10. Liverpool ____________________

It was indeed a long drive. The driver was proud to welcome a visitor to New York. He took the motorway that ran right along the shore, and it was a beautiful ride. The road followed a long curve around the edge of Brooklyn, from Gravesend Bay to Fort Hamilton.

Suddenly Inspector Hudson sat up straight.
The cab driver smiled.
"Gorgeous, isn't it?" the driver asked. "I'm always surprised, myself, and I've seen it a million times."
Inspector Hudson remembered that New Yorkers are known to say "a million" when they mean "a lot".
"Marvelous, really," said Inspector Hudson. He had seen the skyline of New York in pictures, but he had not expected it to be so beautiful in real life.

Übung 26: Setzen Sie das Gegenteil des vorgegebenen Wortes ein!

! ÜBUNG 26

"The entrance to the harbor is called the Narrows," explained the cab driver. "(1. No) Every ______ ship has to pass through this (2. wide) narrow ______ body of water. There's a lot of traffic!"
They drove under a (3. low) high ______ bridge, and the driver gestured upwards. "At the time it was (4. destroyed) built ______, the Verrazano Narrows Bridge was the (5. shortest) longest ______ suspension bridge in the world. They built it when I was a kid. It's hard to believe that before then, you had to (6. come) ~~leave~~ go ______ to Staten Island by ferry."
The cab (7. passenger) driver ______ gestured towards *(toward)* the large, green island across the (8. air) water ______ from Brooklyn.

"I hear the longest suspension bridge is now in England!" he said. "I'll have to go (9. here) ___there___ some day."

A long, low boat whistle sounded. The cab driver (10. cried) ___laughed___.

"There's a lot of traffic on the water, too," he said. "Just like on the highway! The boats blow their horns to try to keep out of one another's way. See that fire boat?"

The cab driver pointed at a small boat shooting up a jet of water like a fountain.

"I wonder what it's celebrating," said the cabbie. "And that's a tug boat escorting an ocean liner into New York Harbor."

Inspector Hudson thought of just how far that ocean liner had come.

"It's a tricky business," said the cab driver. "It's like a lot of what goes on in New York. You need a *license* (licence). For example, the *harbor* (harbour) pilots have a special *license.* You really have to know what you're doing."

The cab driver sighed.

"It can be hard to get permission to operate a taxi, too. It's called a taxi medallion – and it costs a fortune. You have to wonder where all that money is going, you know?"

The cabbie looked at Hudson in the rear view mirror.

"At least that's legal," said the cabbie.

Hudson remembered the rumours *(rumors)* that the Skyline Syndicate controlled many aspects of life in the city. They forced people to pay protection money.

"I let the *boss* worry about things like that. I just drive. I don't know where I would get the kind of money it would take to drive a taxi of my own," said the driver. "I'd have to rob a bank."

Übung 27: Welche Wörter gehören zusammen?

1. protection	☐	station
2. tug	☐	phone
3. suspension	☐	terminal
4. police	☐	booth
5. ocean	☐	bridge
6. cab	☐	constable
7. real	☐	lane
8. petrol	☐	boat
9. mobile	☐	life
10. breakdown	☐	line
11. airline	☐	driver
12. phone	☐	money

He turned on the radio, and upbeat music filled the cab.
"That's the Statue of Liberty," said the cab driver. "Up ahead, that's the Brooklyn Bridge. And all those buildings across the water …"
Inspector Hudson sighed, "The skyline of New York."
"The one and only," smiled the cab driver. "You know, it's funny. When you're over there, you can't see it. The picture postcards are all taken from the Brooklyn side."
The taxicab continued along the curve of the Brooklyn shore. Inspector Hudson could not take his eyes off the skyline. Suddenly, the radio programme *(program)* was interrupted by an announcement.

"This is New York City Police Commissioner Leonard Johnson. Many of you have heard about the armed robbery at the Transatlantic Bank this morning. A security guard was seriously injured. An off-duty police *officer,* John Mahoney, ran to the aid of the guard and was shot by the robbers as they escaped. It is with great regret that I inform you that *Officer* Mahoney died of his wounds this afternoon at 4:15. I know you join me in extending our deepest sympathy to the family of *Officer* Mahoney. The New York Police Department (NYPD) is determined to bring the perpetrators to justice. I am asking every New Yorker to help. If you have any information that would help lead to the arrest of the men who robbed the bank and killed *Officer* Mahoney, please call 1-800-COP-SHOT. That's 1-800-COP-SHOT. Thank you for your cooperation."

"Wow," said the cabbie. "This just became a different ballgame." He switched off the radio.

ÜBUNG 28 !

Übung 28: Finden Sie ein Synonym im Text!

1. gravely __________
2. assistance __________
3. people who did it __________
4. condolences __________
5. injuries __________
6. telephone __________
7. sorrow __________
8. to bring to trial and to punish __________
9. not on duty __________
10. to offer __________

"I saw a bus at the airport," said Inspector Hudson, "with a bumper sticker advertising the telephone number 1-800-COP-SHOT."

"Oh, yes," said the driver. "That's nothing new. Everyone knows the cops don't fool around when a police *officer* is killed. You can bet they are laying down a dragnet for these guys. They'll get them, too."

Übung 29: Ergänzen Sie den Dialog mit den passenden Angaben aus der folgenden Liste!
(nodded, laughed, said the cabbie, asked Inspector Hudson, exclaimed, smiled Inspector Hudson, agreed the cabbie)

"Do you think New Yorkers will call in with information?"

1. ______________________________.

The cab driver 2. __________________________.

"All kinds of *nuts* (nutters) will be calling in," 3. ______________ ____________________, "all claiming they did it. You would not believe the number of deluded people out there. They actually believe they did something terrible. Every time the cops ask for information – bang, they get a million nuts on the phone."

The cabbie thought for a moment.

"I don't know whether it's a power fantasy or a guilt trip."

"I've heard that New York cab drivers are the philosophers of the city," 4. _________________________________. "They must see a lot of life."

"We see it all," 5. ______________________________. "The good and the bad. Myself, I just try to stay out of trouble."

"You seem to know a lot about people, too. But how do you know about such callers?"

The cabbie looked at Hudson in the rear view mirror.

"My wife's sister is a cop," he said.

"I see."

"But I'll tell you something. Anyone who calls in with information about this one is taking his life in his hands. Nobody commits this kind of crime alone. This is a syndicate action."

"The Skyline Syndicate?"

The cabbie 6. ______________________________ silently.

"Let's just say that anybody who sings is taking a big risk. He could wind up just as dead as *Officer* Mahoney."

By this time, the taxi was halfway over the Williamsburg Bridge, high above the river that runs between Brooklyn and Manhattan.

"What a view!" 7. ______________________________ Inspector Hudson.

"It's free, too," said the cabbie. "Courtesy of the City of New York."
Hudson smiled.
"Most people think that Brooklyn is pretty boring," said the cabbie. "Just a lot of ordinary citizens who take the *subway* every day to their jobs in the city."

Übung 30: Setzen Sie den Dialog fort, indem Sie die folgenden Abschnitte in die richtige Reihenfolge bringen!

1. "A lot of banks," smiled the cabbie. "But there are a lot of banks in midtown Manhattan, too."

2. "Technically, the five boroughs are all one big city," said the cabbie. "But those of us who live in the more residential boroughs - Brooklyn, Queens, Staten Island and the Bronx - still call Manhattan 'the city'."

3. "The city?" asked Inspector Hudson. "I thought that the five boroughs of New York were one big city."

4. "The banks?" asked Hudson.

5. Hudson waited for the driver to continue his explanation, as the taxi cruised off the bridge and into the city.

6. "Manhattan is where the power and the money are," explained the cabbie. "Here in downtown Manhattan," he said, as he waved his hand at the crowded streets, "is where you find the courts, the Stock Exchange …"

7. "Now you're talking!" he said. "Yes, we have a million banks. We've got all kinds of banks: banks for merchants, and banks for stockbrokers. We even have banks for banks! Rich people have their own private bankers, and a whole lot of ordinary people just work for the banks."

8. “I suppose you might say that New York has a million banks?” asked Inspector Hudson.

9. The cabbie suddenly frowned.

Lösung: _ _ _ _ _ _ _ _ _ _

Übung 31: Unterstreichen Sie das richtige Wort!

ÜBUNG 31

“Like that poor guy who got hit in the head this morning.”
“The security guard?” 1. laughed/asked Inspector Hudson.
The cabbie 2. nodded/barked. Suddenly he looked Inspector Hudson in the eyes.
“Do you have a special interest in banks?” he 3. asked/exclaimed.
“You might say so,” 4. said/shouted Inspector Hudson.
“What do you do, anyway?” 5. asked/exclaimed the cabbie, looking at Hudson in his rear view mirror.
Hudson decided to tell the truth. The cab driver seemed like an honest working man.
“I’m an inspector at Scotland Yard.”
The cabbie let out a long, low whistle.
“No kidding!” he 6. exclaimed/asked.
“Don’t tell me you’re in the city to investigate – wait! That bank that was robbed this morning was called, how was it called again – ”
“The Transatlantic Bank,” 7. agreed/asked Hudson. “Its partner office is in London. In fact, it’s in the part of London we, too, call ‘the City’.”
“London and New York are both great cities,” mused the cab driver. “But right now I had better pay attention to the traffic.”

Übung 32: Setzen Sie die Verben in die richtige Zeitform!

The cab (1. turn) ______________ into Forty-fourth Street and (2. pull) ______________ up in front of the Ivy Club.

"My nephew (3. impress) ______________. (4. wait) ______________ till I (5. tell) ______________ him that I (6. drive) ______________ you from the airport to the city!"

The cabbie (7. press) ______________ a button on the meter and (8. print) ______________ out a receipt for the charges.

"You wouldn't be (9. kid) ______________ me, now, would you?" asked the cabbie.

Hudson handed the driver the money through a slot in the plastic wall separating the passenger's and the driver's sides of the taxi. He thought for a moment, and reached into his wallet again.
"This is my card," he said, as he handed it to the cabbie. "Please give my regards to your nephew."
The cabbie read the business card aloud.
"Inspector James Hudson, Scotland Yard. Well, if that isn't something. I'm pleased to meet you, Inspector. My name is Arjun Patel."
Inspector Hudson went to shake the cabbie's hand goodbye, before he remembered the plastic wall.
"Is this plastic really bulletproof?" asked Hudson.
"So they tell me," said the driver. "I hope I never have to find out."
The cab driver shook his head and looked seriously at Inspector Hudson.

"You take care, now (look after yourself)," said the cabbie.
The doorman of the Ivy Club stepped over to the cab to take Inspector Hudson's bag.
"Welcome to the Ivy Club, sir," he said.
The clerk at the reception *(desk clerk)* asked for his name.
"Inspector James Hudson."
"Welcome to New York, Inspector Hudson. We understand you are a member of our sister club in London. They faxed us a letter of introduction. We've arranged a room for you on the tenth floor. The *bellhop* ((porter)) will take your bag and show you the facilities."
"I'm in a bit of a hurry," said Inspector Hudson.
"Then let me just say that we have a library, a fitness center, a restaurant and a bar and *grill* (grille). Breakfast is served from seven to ten in the Ivy Room. We hope you will enjoy your stay."
The porter brought Inspector Hudson to his room.
"Here is the light switch, sir. The *water faucets* (taps) may be a bit different from what you are used to in England. The electrical plugs are different, and we use 100 volts AC. Do you need an adapter?"
Inspector Hudson thought that Miss Paddington had probably not thought to pack one.
"Why yes, thank you," said Inspector Hudson.
"If there is anything else, sir, please *call* (ring)," said the porter.

! ÜBUNG 33

Übung 33: Sind die folgenden Wörter britisch, amerikanisch oder beides?

1. desk clerk ____________________
2. porter ____________________
3. ring ____________________

4. faucet ______

5. grill ______

6. constable ______

Inspector Hudson stepped up to the picture windows overlooking Forty-fourth Street. Up and down the street, he saw the large, colourful *(colorful)* flags hanging outside several of the buildings. He recognised ((recognized)) them as the flags of important American universities.

"There are many kinds of power," thought Inspector Hudson. "And there are many forms of powerful organisations ((organizations))."

Inspector Hudson looked all the way down the street to his right. He could just make out Grand Central Station. To his left was the legendary Fifth Avenue.

Hudson had expected to see the skyscrapers for which New York is famous. But Forty-fourth Street was built to a more human scale. The buildings on this street were not all that high, and they were very beautiful.

In the street below, he saw hundreds of people walking. They walked on the pavement *(sidewalks)*, and even in the street. The New Yorkers seemed to cross the street wherever they liked. There were many bright yellow taxicabs, one after another. Lorries double-parked to make deliveries. The traffic flowed slowly but surely, like a huge and very noisy river.

It was a bit of a disappointment to Inspector Hudson that here, in the middle of the city, he could not see the skyline.

"But I'm in the thick of it," he said to himself. "Here I am, in the heart of New York."

A knock at the door interrupted Inspector Hudson's thoughts.

"I brought the adapter, sir," said the porter.

"Could you advise me, please?" asked Inspector Hudson. "I need to get to the offices of the Federal Bureau of Investigation, at this address, as quickly as possible. Should I take a taxicab?" Hudson showed the porter a slip of paper on which Sir Reginald had written an address.

ÜBUNG 34 !

Übung 34: Schreiben Sie die Kurzformen aus!

"Oh, no, sir," smiled the porter. "1. That's ________________ only a couple of blocks away. 2. It's ________________ rush hour, and 3. everyone's ________________ going home from work. 4. You'd ________________ be stuck in traffic. 5. I'd ________________ suggest you walk. 6. It's ________________ the fastest way to get there."

"I see," said Inspector Hudson. "Thank you."
Inspector Hudson shut the door behind the porter and thought, "That's exactly what the robbers must have thought this morning. No wonder there was no evidence of a getaway car. Could it be they simply walked away?"
He looked out the window one last time.
"But where did they go?"
Not a quarter of an hour later *(Barely fifteen minutes later),* Inspector Hudson was checking in with a uniformed security guard in a small lobby. The guard was working behind a thick plastic wall.
The guard pushed Hudson's passport and a visitor's badge back through the grille and spoke through a microphone.
"Please pin this badge to your jacket, sir," said the receptionist.

"*Elevator* (Lift) Number Three will take you directly to the eighth floor, sir."

Once again, Inspector Hudson was surprised that the building was not all that high.

"Of course," he thought, "the FBI would want a building it could secure quickly in an emergency."

The security guard on the eighth floor examined Inspector Hudson's credentials and made a quick call.

"Thank you, sir," he said. "Agent O'Leary will be out immediately."

A door opened down the corridor, and a man walked toward Inspector Hudson, wearing a tired smile. Eugene O'Leary was the Supervisory Special Agent in Charge of Operation Skyline.

Übung 35: Verbinden Sie die Synonyme miteinander!

ÜBUNG 35 !

1. spoke	[3] inspected
2. high	[9] sidewalk
3. examined	[5] education
4. directly	[8] escape
5. training	[7] hallway
6. tired	[2] tall
7. corridor	[4] non-stop
8. getaway	[6] sleepy
9. footpath	[1] talked

Inspector Hudson's detective training took over, as he mentally recorded the man's appearance.

"About 5'11", medium build, wavy grey *(gray)* hair, blue eyes, white *(Caucasian),* fair complexion," thought Inspector Hudson.

Agent O'Leary was wearing a grey suit and a white shirt open at the neck. He had a strange way of fading into the background until he addressed Inspector Hudson in a deep, full voice.
"Welcome to New York. I'm Gene O'Leary." Agent O'Leary extended his hand. "Pleased to meet you."
"Inspector James Hudson. The pleasure is entirely mine, Agent O'Leary."
"Please, call me Gene. What do your friends call you? Jim? Jimmy?"
"James," said Hudson. "They call me James."
Hudson was not accustomed to being addressed by his first name at work. He had heard, though, that Americans are apt to call people they have just met by their first names, or even their nicknames. Hudson thought, "When in Rome, do as the Romans."
"How was your flight?" asked O'Leary.
"Splendid, thank you … er, Gene," answered Hudson. "Thank you very much."
"Your *boss* told me this is your first trip to the United States," said O'Leary. "I'm sorry it had to be for a reason like this. But we are very glad to see you!"

ÜBUNG 36 !

Übung 36: Antworten Sie für Inspector Hudson!

1. Welcome to New York! ______________________
2. How was your flight? ______________________
3. What is your name? ______________________
4. What do your friends call you?

____

5. Is this your first trip to the United States?

____

6. Have you been to New York before?

____

O'Leary opened the door to a large room, where fifteen people were madly working. Many typed away at computers. Photocopy machines ran constantly. Phones were ringing off the hook.

Übung 37: Tragen Sie die richtigen Namen ein!

On one wall was a large diagram of the streets immediately surrounding the Transatlantic Bank's midtown Manhattan office. Off to the side were poster-size photos of the faces of two men. 1. ________________ took them to be 2. ________________ and 3. ________________.

"Welcome to the Operation Skyline," said 4. ________________ ________________.

"This is our ((headquarters)) (incident room). Operation Skyline is an ad hoc task force whose mission is to find the people who robbed the bank this morning, shot a security guard and killed 5. ________________. We also want to find out who is behind these people. You've heard of the 6. ______________________________

____________________?"

"Yes, indeed," said 7. ____________________________.

"We'd been after them long before this morning," said O'Leary. "Last year, we put together a task force to deal with an increase in organized (organised) crime. The task force was made of members of the Federal Bureau of Investigation and the New York City Police Department. As of this morning, we are also working with the Metropolitan Transit Authority (MTA). We look for patterns that could help us identify the work of the Skyline Syndicate, and of its individual members."

Agent O'Leary rubbed his forehead.

"This morning was terrible. It may also be our biggest break."

"How's that?" asked Inspector Hudson.

"I'll answer that question once we're in my office and can hear ourselves think," said O'Leary. "But first, let me introduce you to everyone.

May I have your attention, please," shouted Agent O'Leary. "I'd like to introduce Inspector James Hudson of Scotland Yard."

A cheer went up in the headquarters of Operation Skyline.

"How do you do?" said Inspector Hudson.

The room suddenly fell silent and everyone stared at the visitor. They were not used to such formality.

"What is this, dancing school?" asked someone in the corner of the room.

"That's enough out of you," said Agent O'Leary. "You will give Inspector Hudson your full cooperation in this investigation."

"How do you do?" said someone in a high voice, imitating the British guest.

Übung 38: Was sagen Sie oder tun Sie in den folgenden Situationen?

1. May I introduce Miss Perkins?

2. Hear ye, hear ye! The Sixth Circuit Court is now in session!

3. It's a pleasure to meet you at last.

4. Ladies and gentlemen, the President of the United States!

5. On a reception line, the ambassador says to you, "Good evening."

6. In a bar, someone you don't want to talk to says, "Don't I know you from somewhere?"

Agent O'Leary looked around the room and met the eyes of every *officer*.
"I called Scotland Yard this morning," continued O'Leary, "to ask for their cooperation in finding the criminals who hit the Transatlantic Bank this morning, and are responsible for the death of *Officer* Mahoney. You all know that we believe they are the key to the entire Skyline Syndicate. Well, Sir Reginald, the chief over

there, tells me that Inspector Hudson is the best detective in Scotland Yard."

Another cheer went up.

"So I want you to keep up the good work here while I update Inspector Hudson on what we've got so far," said O'Leary. "Lieutenant LaCapra, would you please come to my office as soon as you are finished there?"

O'Leary and Hudson walked back to O'Leary's office, and he closed the door.

"Have a seat," he said. "This is a little painful to explain."

The Agent put his elbows on the desk and folded his hands.

"I've been tracking the Skyline Syndicate for almost a decade. In the early years, the syndicate was a deadly organization that had a finger in every pie. Everywhere there was big money to be made, there they were."

"I read about your work on the case involving the Southside Post Office," remembered Hudson.

ÜBUNG 39 !

Übung 39: Setzen Sie die Verben in die Vergangenheitsform!

"Corruption in the construction industry (1. is) ________________ a major problem, as you undoubtedly (2. read) ________________. But when we (3. prove) ________________ in court that the Skyline Syndicate (4. fix) ______________ the bids for the job, we were able to put away seven of the biggest names in the Skyline Syndicate. With the leaders in jail, the Skyline Syndicate never (5. recover) ________________. At least, not until now."

Agent O'Leary patted his jacket pocket. "Excuse me," he said. "It's an old habit. I (6. stop) ______________ smoking a few months ago." He (7. smile) ______________ wryly at Inspector Hudson.

"In the past few months, I've seen signs of new life in the Skyline Syndicate. Something is happening there, and I don't know what. I've tried to convince my superiors that we absolutely must nip this in the bud. We cannot let the Skyline Syndicate grow back to its former strength."

"And?"

"It's expensive, James. It takes a lot of money to carry out this kind of investigation. And money is exactly what the city doesn't have these days."

"There are cutbacks everywhere," said Hudson.

"Here's the part that's hard to say. As soon as a police *officer* is killed, the entire city is mobilized (mobilised). The public is suddenly on your side. So are the politicians. As of four o'clock this afternoon, we are rolling in *dough* ((money))."

Hudson nodded. "Why not make the best use of it? The money will help provide the resources we need to find the robbers, and break the Syndicate. It's the best memorial we could create for *Officer* Mahoney, and it sounds like the entire city would be relieved to be rid of the Skyline Syndicate."

There was a knock at the door, and a uniformed police *officer* entered. Agent O'Leary's face brightened.

"Allow me to introduce Lieutenant LaCapra of the New York Police Department."

"About 5'8", slim build, thick brown hair, brown eyes, white, olive complexion, appears to be Italian," Hudson thought. "Female."

Übung 40: Welche Wörter stehen in Zusammenhang miteinander?

1. blue	☐ complexion
2. curly	☐ 8 inches
3. slim	☐ build
4. fair	☐ gender
5. female	☐ eyes
6. 5 feet	☐ hair

Hudson extended his hand and said, "Inspector James Hudson, Scotland Yard."

"Looey Looey, NYPD."

Hudson looked confused.

"It's a joke, sir," she said. "But it is what they call me. I'm a lieutenant. Around here, a lieutenant is called a 'looey' – and my first name is Louise. Everybody calls me 'Looey Looey'."

"Ah," said Hudson. "That is the rank we pronounce, 'leftenant'."

It was Looey Looey's turn to look confused.

"So what do they call people?" she asked. "'Lefty'?"

Everyone laughed. Agent O'Leary asked, "Would you like some coffee? I know Looey Looey takes hers black, with sugar."

O'Leary reached over to his coffee machine.

"Might you have some tea ((Do you have any tea))?" asked Hudson.

Agent O'Leary smiled just a bit. "I should have known," he said. "What kind do you prefer?"

"Earl Grey, if you please," said Hudson. "But I'd be happy to drink Darjeeling."

Agent O'Leary pushed the intercom button.

"O'Leary," he said. "Sergeant, would you send down to that health food store for some tea for Inspector Hudson? Get Earl Grey if you can, or Darjeeling."

There was a pause.
"E-A-R-L-G-R-E-Y," said O'Leary, and rang off.
"Lieutenant LaCapra has been analyzing (analysing) the area immediately around the bank," explained Agent O'Leary. "She has plotted every possible escape route. She has also put a lot of thought into the particulars of *ATM machines*."
"Cashpoint machines?"
"Right."
"It's difficult to remember life before cashpoint machines," said Hudson. "They have changed the nature of banking in many ways – at least, in the experience of individual customers who simply want convenient access to cash."
"It's changed the nature of bank robbery, too, sir, if I may say so," said Looey Looey. "ATM machines are often located outside the heavily secured area of a bank. They have to be, in order to be convenient."
There was a knock at the door.
"Here's the tea, *Boss* (sir)," said a sergeant. "And we were out of petty cash, so I stopped at the – "
"ATM machine," guessed O'Leary.
The sergeant closed the door, and the smell of Earl Grey tea filled O'Leary's office.
"ATM machines are convenient," continued Looey Looey, "but they're vulnerable. They are a whole new kind of crime, just waiting to happen."

Übung 41: Übersetzen Sie ins Deutsche!

ÜBUNG 41 !

1. May I see your credit card, please?

2. Where is the nearest cashpoint machine, please?

____

3. I forgot my PIN number!

____

4. Enter your account number now.

____

5. Press two for German.

____

6. Enter your password now.

____

7. Please remove your card.

____

"Would you like a cookie (Would you care for a biscuit)?" asked O'Leary.

Inspector Hudson took one, and saying, "I'd love a biscuit."

"We don't have any *biscuits* (rolls)," said Looey Looey. "But we've got some *donuts* (doughnuts) next door."

"Wait!" said O'Leary. "I know the answer to this one! What we call *cookies*, the English call biscuits."

"Quite *((that's right)),*" said Inspector Hudson, swallowing his biscuit.

"I think I'll get a *donut*," said Looey Looey.

"Do you want one, *Boss*?"

"No, thanks," said O'Leary. "I'm going to order dinner soon. But would you bring Peter Stanley back with you, please?"

"Sure thing, *Boss*," said Looey Looey.
O'Leary offered the box to Inspector Hudson again.
"Would you, ah, care for another biscuit, James?"
"Why, thank you," said Inspector Hudson.

Übung 42: Übersetzen Sie ins Englische!

1. Möchten Sie ein Stück Gebäck?

2. Ich hätte gerne ein Kännchen Kaffee.

3. Ich hätte lieber eine Tasse Tee.

4. Haben Sie heute Schokoladenkuchen?

5. Ich hätte gerne sechs Berliner.

6. Kann ich bitte ein Glas Wasser haben?

7. Gibt es noch etwas Warmes?

Looey Looey returned holding a chocolate-covered pastry, and followed by a man in a different sort of uniform.

"About 5'9, muscular build, light brown hair, blue eyes, white, fair complexion," thought Hudson. "The uniform looks familiar."

"Inspector Hudson, I'd like you to meet Assistant Chief Constable Peter Stanley of Merseyside. Peter, may I introduce Inspector James Hudson of Scotland Yard."

"How do you do," said Chief Stanley.

"How do you do," replied Inspector Hudson, as he rose to his feet in surprise.

"Chief Stanley is visiting from the police department in Liverpool," said Agent O'Leary. "He has been here for two weeks. In turn, the NYPD sent someone to train over there. It's called cross-deputizing (cross-deputising)."

"What a splendid ((great)) idea," exclaimed Inspector Hudson.

"Indeed ((It certainly is))," confirmed Chief Stanley. "It's particularly important in areas that require international cooperation."

"That way," continued Agent O'Leary, "in case of an emergency, some people in the United States are already familiar with how things are done in the United Kingdom – and vice versa."

"We also compare procedures," said Chief Stanley, "to see how we might improve police procedures in each country."

"Jolly good idea *(Great idea),*" said Inspector Hudson.

"Consider yourself a case in point," replied Agent O'Leary.

ÜBUNG 43 !

Übung 43: Sind die folgenden Ausdrücke der Zustimmung britisch, amerikanisch oder beides?

1. Jolly good show! ____________________
2. Great idea! ____________________

3. Indeed! ______

4. Brilliant! ______

5. Okay! ______

6. That sounds good! ______

7. Splendid! ______

"Back in Liverpool, my job includes the areas of Major Crime, and Intelligence and Security Issues. International cooperation is very important in these areas, and in prosecuting organised ((organized)) crime," said Chief Stanley. "That is my special interest."
"Please have a seat," said Agent O'Leary. "I called in Chief Stanley to report on his work of the last weeks. He can tell you why we suspect that the bank robbery is tied to the Skyline Syndicate."
"Can I ask something first?" said Looey Looey.
"What is it?" asked O'Leary. She turned to the two Englishmen.
"Why didn't either of you answer the question?"
They looked at her blankly.
"What question?" asked Chief Stanley.
"How you are doing," she said.
"I beg your pardon?" asked Inspector Hudson.
"Well, first Chief Stanley asked, 'How do you do' – and then you said exactly the same thing!"

Übung 44: Bilden Sie ein Adverb!

ÜBUNG 44 !

Stanley and Hudson smiled (1. polite) ______.

They seemed (2. slight) ______ embarrassed.

"Well," said Hudson, (3. quiet) ______________________. "I didn't mean to pry."

"I just met the bloke ((guy))!" said Stanley.

"It would seem too personal," said Hudson, looking aside.

"'How do you do' is just something we say when we are introduced to one another."

"In that case," said Looey (4. point) ______________________, "you might want to know that around here, if someone asks how you are doing, they expect an answer," said Looey Looey. "It can be short, but it has to be an answer. Like this," she said, turning (5. drama) ______________________ to Agent O'Leary.

"How are you doing, *Boss*?" she asked O'Leary.

"Pretty well. *Yourself* ((And you))?"

"Fine, thanks," said Looey Looey, (6. casual) ______________________.

The two Englishmen laughed again at the show.
"Is that why everyone stared at me when I was introduced?" asked Inspector Hudson.
"Well, that and a few other things," admitted Looey Looey.
"I'll try to keep it in mind," said Inspector Hudson.
"Now that everyone is doing fine, could we please move on to business?" asked Agent O'Leary. "I've asked Peter in to tell us about his work on the Skyline Syndicate."
"As I was saying, the bit ((part)) that interests me the most is organised crime," said Constable Stanley. "It sounds glamourous *(glam-*

orous), but most of my work is data analysis. I came to New York to analyse data about the group that calls itself the Skyline Syndicate."

"In my line of work," stressed Constable Stanley, "we have a motto: 'Follow the money'."

Inspector Hudson nodded.

"The crimes these organisations commit are unspeakable," said Stanley. "The power struggles within the organisations are also just awful."

Stanley sighed.

"Please don't misunderstand me. I mean no disrespect, and especially not to the late *Officer* Mahoney. But in the end, for the leaders of organised crime, the robberies and even the murders are not what it's about. They're in it for the money."

Agent O'Leary looked grim.

"Our most powerful weapon in the fight against organised crime is pattern recognition," said Constable Stanley. "I look for patterns. When I see changes in a pattern, I suspect something is in the works."

"I see," said Hudson.

"It's not as dramatic as a car chase," admitted Stanley. "I admire the constables who are out there digging up information, but I'm a quieter type. I took a course in computer science *(I studied computer science).* I look at what all of our front-line people are doing, and I run calculations to try and find out what the connections are."

Übung 45: Setzen Sie, wenn nötig, die fehlende Präpositionen ein!

1. I have a master's degree __________ science.

2. I studied __________ geology.

3. I am writing a dissertation ___on___ the poetry of John Milton.

4. I'd like to learn ______ French.

5. I took a course ___in___ maths *(math)*.

6. Did you do well ___on___ the test?

7. At the moment, Hudson is working ___on___ a very interesting case.

8. Could you please put me ___through to___ Agent O'Leary?

9. I left my umbrella ___at___ work.

"He also tries to guess what might happen next," said Agent O'Leary.
Inspector Hudson looked sharply at Stanley.
"The two areas most important for my analyses," explained Stanley, "are the flow of money, and the pattern of violent crime."
Agent O'Leary looked over at Inspector Hudson. Hudson's eyes were closing.
"It looks like it's about time to break for dinner," said O'Leary. "I think we're losing the Inspector here."
Hudson's eyes snapped open.
"I did warn you that my line of work is a bit duff ((boring))," said Stanley. "It's mainly statistics."
"I'm dreadfully ((very)) sorry," Hudson apologised ((apologized)). "I can't explain it. I feel like someone hit me over the head."
"Jet lag," observed Looey Looey. "Remember, it's after midnight in Blimey Town."
"Lieutenant," said O'Leary sharply.

"If you mean 'England', Looey, it's called 'Blightey'," added Stanley helpfully.
"But I've been up past midnight before," said Hudson. "I know that many people consider my habits old-fashioned, but – "
"But jet lag is like being up past midnight on another planet," said Looey Looey. "Maybe you need some coffee."
Hudson took another sip of Earl Grey tea.
"Would you like to have something hot to eat, after your long trip?" asked O'Leary.
"No, thank you. I can hardly think about eating."
"We're losing him fast," said Looey Looey.
"I'm going to ask Sergeant Vélez to escort you back to the Ivy Club," said Agent O'Leary. "We can continue this in the morning. There is no sense making you sick with jet lag. We are very grateful that you have come all this way to help with the investigation. We want you in good shape."
Hudson was grateful for their concern. The door to O'Leary's office was opened next by a man in the dark blue uniform of the NYPD. Hudson could barely think: "About 5'10, muscular build, curly brown hair, brown eyes, Hispanic, dark complexion."
"Goodnight," everyone said.
"Thank you so much," said Inspector Hudson.
"See you in the morning," said Agent O'Leary. "Whenever you feel up to it, come over. There's always someone here, twenty-four hours a day. The security desk downstairs has your name on file."

Inspector Hudson woke up feeling much better.
"What nice curtains they have here at the Ivy Club," he thought. "They effectively block out all the light so that the guests can sleep." He reached over to shut off his alarm clock, which had not yet rung.

"I can't believe it!" he exclaimed. "It's only three o'clock in the morning!"
Hudson groaned and sat up. "Of course, it's nine a.m. in London," he thought. "I'd be at Scotland Yard already, if this were an ordinary day."
Then he remembered that this was no ordinary day. It all came back: the Skyline Syndicate, the armed robbery, a police *officer* dead … and everyone at headquarters looking to him to solve the case.
"Why, oh why, did Sir Reginald think I would be of any use in New York?" wondered Hudson. "The entire city is a puzzle to me!"
Hudson shut off his alarm clock and decided to make the best of it. "Perhaps today we'll have a bit more to go on."

! ÜBUNG 46

Übung 46: Was sagt man in den folgenden Situationen zur Verabschiedung?

1. A general dismisses his troops after a war.
2. A student leaves the library at midnight.
3. You are a woman, and your date just brought you home.
4. You ring off *(You hang up)*.
5. You kiss your five-year-old nephew.
6. You part from your colleagues after an evening seminar.

☐ See you in the morning.
☐ Good night.
☐ Farewell.
☐ Sleep tight!
☐ Goodbye.
☐ I had a lovely evening.

Übung 47: Welche Wörter haben etwas mit der Zeit zu tun? Unterstreichen Sie!

Half an hour later, he was back at the task force headquarters.
"Good morning, Sergeant," he said to the woman at the front desk as he showed her his identification.
"Good morning, Inspector. They told me you might be in early."
"You all seem to have more experience with jet lag than I do," replied Inspector Hudson.
"Would you like some coffee, sir?"
"He'd like tea, if I'm not mistaken, Sergeant."
A familiar voice farther down the corridor let Hudson know that Looey Looey was on the job.
The sergeant picked up an unfamiliar packet next to the coffee machine and sniffed.
"Earl Grey," Looey Looey told the sergeant. "Get used to it."
Looey Looey picked up another packet.
"But he might want this one in the morning." She read the second label aloud: "'English Breakfast Tea'. We've got you covered, Inspector."

Hudson smiled. Looey Looey might sound a bit rough at the edges, he thought, but she noticed and remembered everything. Her presence on this task force suggested that her investigative skills were prized by all the other police *officers.* And it was very kind of her to hunt down *(scout up)* the tea. Hudson felt more at home already.
"Anything new?" he asked.
"It's been dead around here," she replied. "We had nothing better to do than take bets on what you eat for breakfast."
Hudson could barely swallow his tea before laughing.

ÜBUNG 48 !

Übung 48: Unterstreichen Sie alles Essbare!

"Here's the list." Looey picked up a piece of paper. "Two bets on bacon and eggs. Five for English muffins."
Hudson laughed again.
"Jones said he thought you would eat porridge. Vélez said to put her down for porridge, too, because she didn't know what it was."
"Do I seem that alien to you?"
"Would you like some scrambled tofu?"
"I must confess, I – "
"It's alright, Inspector Hudson. This is New York. You can order anything. If you want scrambled tofu, it will be here in five minutes."
"Eggs and rashers would be perfect," decided Inspector Hudson. "With toast and orange marmalade."

"I'm sure we can get those rashers, sir, if you would just please tell me what they are."
"I believe you say 'bacon'."
"We have a winner," announced Looey Looey to the entire room. "Inspector Hudson has just ordered bacon and eggs for breakfast. Two lucky police *officers* will split the pot. That would be Sergeant Ozbek and myself. For your further information, people in England call bacon 'rashers'."
Sergeant Ozbek rolled his eyes. A few tired people clapped their hands.
"I've got an idea," said Looey. "I need a break from this elegant location. Let's go downstairs for breakfast. There's a coffee shop down the block that's open all night. Then we can walk over to Grand Central Station. Agent O'Leary asked me to take you around the neighborhood to see if you notice anything we haven't picked

up. We might as well go now. By the time we finish looking around a bit, it will be just about five o'clock, which is when the robbery took place."

Übung 49: Bringen Sie die durcheinander geratenen Buchstaben in die richtige Reihenfolge!

As they left the coffee shop, Looey Looey looked at her watch.

"It's still early, Inspector. I have an idea. Let's go over to Grand Central Station first, while it's still (1. osdelc) ______________."

They walked east, toward one of the biggest transportation centres *(centers)* in the city. It was still (2. qtiue) ______________ dark, though the sky was lightening just a bit.

"Every (3. gnhit) ______________, Grand Central closes between 1:30 and 5 a.m.," Looey Looey explained. "The last commuter train to the suburbs north of the city leaves at exactly 1:30. Every (4. sgelin) ______________ night, there are dramas over here. There are always some (5. leopep) ______________ who miss the train. They never learn! You would think they change the schedule every day of the week!"

Looey Looey waved her hands. "Maybe they should ring a bell in certain bars (6. dauron) ______________ here … It's really none of my business, sir, but … well, we just want to make sure that (7. ynbood) ______________________ gets hurt wandering around here in the (8. ddilem) ______________________ of the night."

"Like last night."
"Precisely."
Inspector Hudson looked up at the enormous stone building looming over Forty-second Street.
"What an impressive building."
They walked around to the office of the Stationmaster.
"I'm Lieutenant LaCapra of the NYPD," she said, showing her identification.
"And this is Inspector Hudson of Scotland Yard. We're here on official business."
"My, my, Lieutenant," said the Stationmaster, checking their identification. "To what do we owe the *honor* (honour)? The station is closed, you know."
"Yes, sir. We're working on that bank robbery from yesterday."
"The one where …?"
"Yes, sir. We're thinking about possible escape routes the robbers might have used. I'd like to give Inspector Hudson a feel for the major transportation centers of the city – the places where a number of *subway* and commuter lines come together. I explained to Inspector Hudson that there are no Metro North trains at this time of night."
"We use this time to clean the station and, well, we also like to avoid trouble." The Stationmaster walked them into the famous lobby, where a grand old clock had kept time for generations of New Yorkers dashing for trains.

Looey Looey pointed up at the blue ceiling painted with golden stars. “It’s a miniature world in here, with its own heaven. See the constellations?”
“They’re all in transit, too,” observed the Inspector. “The stars, like the commuters, have their fixed routes across the sky.”
“The stars were awfully hard to see for several decades,” remarked the Stationmaster. “The ceiling was cleaned and renovated some years ago, and for the first time, people of my generation could see the sky, so to speak.”
“Look over here,” said the Stationmaster. “See that solid black square on the ceiling?” He pointed to a blank moment in the sky.
“They left that patch,” he explained, “as a reminder of what the ceiling looked like before it was restored.”
“There must be an incredible amount of traffic in the station,” said Inspector Hudson, “to have generated that kind of dirt.”
“When it’s empty like this, it’s hard to believe that we could possibly need all this space. But once the trains start running again at 5:40, you won’t recognize (recognise) the place. Half a million people a day pass through Grand Central Station. That’s why we take the time to scrub the place down during these quiet hours.”

Übung 50: Ersetzen Sie die Wörter durch Zahlen und die Zahlen durch Wörter!

ÜBUNG 50 !

1. 5:40 ______________________

2. 500,000 ______________________

3. one o’clock ______________________

4. six in the evening ______________________

5. two fifteen ______________________

6. half past seven ______________________

7. quarter after/past eight ______________________

Suddenly, a piercing wail filled the enormous dome.
"EEEEEEEeeeeeeeeeeeek! Help! Help!"
The scream reverberated so in the empty building that it was difficult to tell where it was coming from.
"There!" shouted the Stationmaster. "A cleaning lady was working down by Platform One! You two run down there! I must run back to my headquarters!"
Looey Looey and Inspector Hudson were already running as fast as they could in the direction of the scream. They found a woman standing alone in a hallway, screaming and screaming. There was no one else around, until two Metropolitan Transit Authority police *officers* turned the corner, out of breath.
"What's wrong, ma'am?" they asked frantically. Looey Looey ran up and down the corridor, looking in all directions to see if someone had escaped.
"Did someone hurt you? What happened?"
The woman grabbed the arm of one of the MTA *patrol officers* and babbled in a mixture of English and Spanish.
"She says it's in the *men's room* (gents)," said one of the MTA *cops* (bobbies).
The second *patrol officer* drew a gun and stepped to the side of the door to the gents.
"Is anyone there?" he shouted. "Put down your weapons! Come out with your hands up!"
The second *patrol office*r spoke up. "She says it's dead."
"What's dead?"

"The leg."
The woman now moaned in a low voice. The second *patrol officer* spoke to her in Spanish.
"She found it in the *garbage* (rubbish)," he said. "Inside the garbage container was another plastic *garbage bag* (bin liner)."
The woman continued in a strange, low voice.
"The second bag was open at the top. When she picked up the big bag …"
The woman spoke three more words and began to scream again.
"She saw the foot."
"Is there anyone in there?" repeated the *patrol officer* by the gents.
He burst through with his pistol ready to fire. The room was empty.
His voice came through the door.
"I think you'd better take a look."

Übung 51: Sind die folgende Ausdrücke britisch, amerikanisch oder beides? Übersetzen Sie!

ÜBUNG 51 !

1. Bin it! ______

2. Tip the pieces into the rubbish. ______

______

3. Take out the trash! ______

______

4. dustman ______

5. bin liner ______

6. garbage truck ______

His partner stayed with the cleaning woman, and Inspector Hudson walked through the door. They emerged together a moment later, looking ill.

"It doesn't smell too good, Jack," said the *patrol officer* to his partner. "It's just like the lady said."

Looey Looey was already on her mobile with *precinct* (constabulary) headquarters. Jack pulled out his phone to alert the Stationmaster.

"Just be glad this isn't rush hour," said the first *patrol officer.*

"Actually," sighed Looey Looey, "the doors just opened."

ÜBUNG 52 !

Übung 52: Setzen Sie die passenden Wörter aus der folgenden Liste in die Lücken ein!

(leftover, straggled, joined, unfortunate, stared, businessmen, worse, party)

The first knot of people who 1. ______________ in looked like the diehards who had missed their trains and decided to tough it out on the street until five. Their 2. ______________ clothes were a bit 3. ______________ for wear. A dozen or so freshly-dressed but sleepy-eyed 4. ______________ followed, heading for the coffee stands that would open soon. The 5. ______________ party people were headed for the restrooms when a dozen police *officers* in NYPD blue suddenly burst through the main door on the run. The early morning commuters 6. ______________ as the cops were

7. ______________________ by six pairs of MTA *patrol officers,* all converging on the scene of the 8. ______________________ discovery.

"My goodness, what a crowd," murmured Inspector Hudson.
"They're a little touchy, these last years," said Jack. "As soon as something unusual happens, they respond in force."
Two cops started marking off the area with yellow and black crime scene tape. No one would be allowed near the scene of the crime.
"What are you doing, letting people in here?" yelled the NYPD lieutenant.
The ranking MTA *officer* remained calm. "I'm Chief Daniels of the Metropolitan Transit Authority. As far as we know, this discovery poses no danger to the thousands of people who will be pouring through this station in half an hour, trying to get to work. Your people are already sealing off the area. You're telling me you want to lock Grand Central Station? *No way!* ((Out of the question!)) What do you want people to think, there's a nuclear war?"
"Can I use the *bathroom* (toilet)?" asked a man in a dinner jacket *(tuxedo),* who had just walked up.
"No!" screamed the police lieutenant.
"Get out of here! ((Go away!))"
"Well, excuse me!" screamed back the well-dressed man. "This station belongs to the people of New York, and I am reporting you to my congresswoman!"
"I'm sorry, sir," said Jack in a soothing voice, stepping over to the man, who had clearly had too much champagne, both before and after missing the 1:30 train to the suburbs.
"We have an emergency here." He kept talking as he steered the man in another direction.

Übung 53: Finden Sie die passende Antwort!

1. This is an emergency.	2	We are closed.
2. I'm sorry, sir.	5	That way!
3. Where are the ladies' toilets?	4	There's another one at six.
4. We'll miss the train!	3	First door to the right.
5. Which way did he go?	6	I'll get out my dinner jacket.
6. Tonight's dinner is black tie.	1	Please remain calm.

The two *patrol officers* kept quietly taping.
The lieutenant in blue kept right on yelling.
"You have no idea what kind of dangerous situation you might have here! This could be a deadly menace!"
"He's already dead!" screamed the MTA *officer,* losing his temper. "This guy is beyond being a menace!"
"Excuse me, gentlemen," said Inspector Hudson. "I am Inspector Hudson of Scotland Yard." He produced his identification.
"And who is this *nut case* (nutter)?" screamed the lieutenant. "Is he with the guy in the *tuxedo* (dinner jacket)?"
Inspector Hudson simply stood there with his card out.
"He really is from Scotland Yard," said Looey Looey. "I'm Lieutenant LaCapra, NYPD. He's working with me on that robbery from yesterday."
Looey Looey's blue uniform seemed to calm down her fellow *officer.* He reached for Inspector Hudson's identification.
"Just what we need," he muttered. "Jack the Ripper."
"We were about to leave," continued Looey Looey. "We were just waiting for you to arrive. Would you give us a call as soon as you wrap this up?" She handed him her card, with the phone number of the task force headquarters. "We'd really appreciate it."
Back on Forty-second Street, Looey Looey let out a long breath.

"Do you think they'll stop bickering long enough to bag that corpse?"
"I wouldn't have thought you were the peace-keeping type," said Inspector Hudson.
"Well, it helped to have an inspector from Scotland Yard on hand. That distracted everyone long enough to take their minds off of who was going to play the *Boss*," laughed Looey Looey.
"That reminds me," said Inspector Hudson. "May I ask you about the term *'Boss'*? I hear it often at headquarters. To my ears, it sounds a bit disrespectful."
"I wouldn't use it anywhere outside a *police headquarters* (constabulary headquarters), that's for sure," said Looey Looey. "But among us, it's a way of acknowledging rank. There are so many fine gradations of rank that it's simpler just to call everyone above you *'Boss'*. People of similar rank might call one another by their first names, but …" She paused. "Well, in your case, I had the feeling you were the 'sir' type."
It crossed Hudson's mind that if things were different, he wouldn't mind being called 'James'.
"I'm a special case," she continued. "When people call me 'Looey' for short – well, some of them mean 'Lieutenant', and some of them mean 'Louise'."
Hudson was left to pondern this as they crossed a busy street.

Übung 54: Wie reden sie Ihren Vorgesetzten an?

1. Inspector Hudson calls his supervisor
a) ☐ Mr Reginald.
b) ☐ Reginald.
c) ☐ Sir Reginald.

ÜBUNG 54 !

2. Miss Paddington calls her employer
a) ☐ Mr Hudson.
b) ☐ Mr Inspector.
c) ☐ James.

3. Looey Looey calls her superior
a) ☐ Sir.
b) ☐ Chief O'Leary.
c) ☐ *Boss*.

4. Sergeant Özbek calls his superior
a) ☐ Ma'am.
b) ☐ *Boss*.
c) ☐ Sir.

5. The porter calls the club guests
a) ☐ *Boss*.
b) ☐ You.
c) ☐ Sir.

"I already told Agent O'Leary on the phone that we're taking a detour," Looey said. "They won't have any information on that leg for a while yet, so I thought I'd take you by the scene of the crime yesterday. There isn't much to see in the lobby, but I'll show you the *subway* entrance that is right near the bank."

Looey pointed at the dark green entrance, marked with several letters and numbers.

"That's how I think the robbers made their getaway. I mean, where else could they have gone? That's assuming they didn't take a car," said Looey Looey.

"Can you rule out a car?"

"No, sir. But if you know anything about the city, you know that a car would be an awfully big risk. Early in the morning, there are a lot of trucks in the city, making deliveries. If one truck were blocking the street, your getaway car would be trapped."

Hudson remembered the trucks he had seen from the windows of his room at the Ivy Club. They were unloading everything from toothpaste to oranges to wallpaper.

"Ten million people need a lot of supplies," he realised ((realized)).

"Including cash, sir."

They looked at one another.

"A lot of cash. And here's where they get it," said Looey. They looked across the street to the midtown offices of the Transatlantic Bank. Over the entry hung a navy blue flag with three white lines like ocean waves.

"The Transatlantic Bank has been in business since the eighteenth century," observed Inspector Hudson. "This bank must have financed many sailing expeditions to what is now the United States. Britain has always been a naval power."

"As in, 'Britania, rule the waves', sir?"

Hudson smiled.

"It's your country now," he conceded.

"And it was discovered by an Italian," she insisted. "At least, this part was. Verrazano sailed into New York Harbor. You saw the Verrazano Narrows Bridge on your way into the city?"

"An unforgettable sight."

"Some day you'll travel to New England, sir. Verrazano also landed on Block Island, and he even sailed into Newport Harbor. Of course, he was shown the way by the local residents."

"And I am equally grateful for your tour of midtown Manhattan."

Hudson decided not to mention that the Italian explorer had been sent by the King of France.

ÜBUNG 55 !

Übung 55: Wer war wo in der neuen Welt?

1. Verrazano	☐	nowhere
2. Henry Hudson	☐	Newport Bay
3. Inspector Hudson	☐	Grand Central Station
4. Arjun Patel	☐	Brooklyn
5. Narragansett Tribe	☐	New York Harbor
6. the King of France	☐	Hudson River

"Here's the detailed part," Looey said, earnestly. "See there? The entrance is very close to the corner, on the uptown side of the crosstown street. The avenue is a one-way street, and the traffic goes downtown. The *subway* entrance is right outside. My guess is that the robbers waited either around the corner on the crosstown street, or on the stairway to the *subway,* out of sight. They knew exactly when that *armored* (armoured) vehicle would arrive. When they heard the door to the van slam, they went into action."

"Weren't there two security guards to deliver the money?"

"Everyone is cutting costs these days, sir. That's why, unbelievable as it sounds, he was sent out alone. The guards get paid very well, sir – but they're taking their life in their hands."

Hudson frowned, thinking of the guard lying in hospital. "And *Officer* Mahoney?"

ÜBUNG 56 !

Übung 56: Welche der folgenden Paare reimen sich? Markieren Sie mit richtig ✔ oder falsch –!

1. lying, dying ☐
2. good, food ☐
3. find, mind ☐

4. bite, night ☐
5. guess, less ☐
6. worse, verse ☐
7. yard, guard ☐
8. knew, queue ☐
9. street, meat ☐
10. trap, cab ☐
11. where, care ☐

"My guess is that he was walking over from Times Square, on the next cross street downtown. He turned onto the avenue here, and saw the robbery in progress. The crosstown blocks are short, as you see. He ran to the aid of the security guard. He was about thirty feet from the entrance to the bank when he was shot. He dropped on the spot."

"Was he armed?"

"His service revolver was drawn. But we don't just shoot people, sir. We are required to warn them. He probably yelled, 'Stop or I'll shoot!'"

"Yes?"

"And the robbers shot him first. His revolver was never fired."

Hudson looked out over the avenue, which was beginning to fill with cars and people, all on their way to work.

"He was only twenty-three, sir. Six months out of Police Academy."

"I'm very sorry."

"The autopsy showed that he had been drinking, but not more than you would expect of a young man out on the town."

The light turned green. Looey and Hudson crossed the street toward the Transatlantic Bank. Hudson noted the yellow and black stripes on a piece of a plastic crime scene tape that had blown into a corner. He thought back to the scene at Grand Central Station.

ÜBUNG 57 !

Übung 57: Setzen Sie die richtigen Präpositionen ein!

"This is a pretty lively couple of precincts," said Looey, as if 1. ________ cue. "Grand Central, Times Square, and 2. ________ between – a whole lot 3. ________ money."

They stepped 4. ______ the lobby of the bank. There were four cashpoint machines. 5. ______ front of each machine, half a dozen people queued 6. ______ to withdraw money.

"Need any cash, Inspector?" Looey quipped. "Sorry. I guess that wasn't even funny." Inspector Hudson's eyes travelled upward. "That's the surveillance camera?"

"That's right. As you've already seen, the video was taken from that point of view."

Hudson and Looey looked back toward the door, playing the video-tape in their minds.

"They didn't even get this far," said Inspector Hudson. "We might as well take a look at the Underground." He made a note of the angle of the camera. Now he understood that the entrance to the Tube lay just beyond the limits of the camera's lens.

They stepped out into the morning light. The avenue looked like a long, bright yellow streak, as dozens of taxis drove downtown. It was incredible what a difference a few minutes made in the number of people hurrying up and down the streets. A traffic light on the avenue turned red. Looey followed his gaze.

"Once it's after six o'clock," she confirmed, "you'd have millions of witnesses. Well, dozens, sir."

Four NYPD constables had appeared. They were standing at each corner of the street crossing, ready to hand out flyers asking for information about the crimes. Hudson and Looey looked down the long flight of stairs into the Tube.

Übung 58: Geben Sie zu folgenden Wörtern die britische Schreibweise an!

ÜBUNG 58 !

1. tire ____________________
2. favorite ____________________
3. traveled ____________________
4. honor ____________________
5. savor ____________________
6. labor ____________________
7. license ____________________
8. center ____________________

"We're just out of range of the bank's surveillance camera," observed Hudson. "Is there another one downstairs?"

"There are surveillance cameras at every location where money changes hands. This entrance doesn't have what we used to call a *'token booth',*" explained Looey, "and so it's not covered by a surveillance camera."

"So the robbers might have ripped off their masks here, put the money bags in their backpacks, and calmly taken the next train out."

"That's pretty much it, sir. And the trains leave every minute."

"Now to the interesting question," said Hudson. "Where did they go?"

Hudson and Looey walked down past the numbers and letters painted on the wall: “4-5-6-7-S.”

“I take it those are the different *subway* lines that stop here?” Inspector Hudson asked.

“Correct. The 7 and the shuttle go west across town to Times Square, which is the biggest *subway* station in New York. The 4, 5 and 6 lines go uptown and downtown. Once you’re in the *subway* here, you can also walk underground to Grand Central Station – and you’ve seen how big that is.”

Looey pointed to the right. “The 7 also goes east from here. It stops at Grand Central and then heads directly to Queens. Within a couple of stops, you could transfer to one of almost half a dozen lines that run through Queens.”

“So they might have headed almost anywhere.”

“That is basically it, sir.”

ÜBUNG 59 !

Übung 59: Gangsterjagd in New York – beantworten Sie die Fragen!

1. In which borough of the City of New York are we looking for the robbers? ______

2. This borough is divided from north to south into three “parts of town”. What are they?

______

3. In what part of town are Looey and Hudson now?

______

4. Does Times Square lie east or west of Grand Central Station?

5. Which trains go across town from Grand Central Station to Times Square?

6. In which directions do trains number 4, 5 and 6 go?

They looked at one another and shook their heads. They headed down into the maze of platforms and corridors. Together, they walked through every route the robbers might have taken before getting onto a train, until they were right back at Grand Central Station.

"If they were smart, they would have split up," said Hudson wearily. "There are enough escape routes here for a dozen robbers."

"That was the problem, sir. Even though we got the call from the bank almost immediately, we first assumed they had taken off in a car. Too many movies, I guess. It was only a minute or so before we thought of the *subway* – but sir, we couldn't shut down five different *subway* lines in two directions each! People would have panicked! Just think of the trains backed up throughout the city!"

Hudson remembered that Chief Daniels, the MTA *officer* this morning, had made the same point. He refused to shut down Grand Central Station because they had found part of a corpse.

Looey continued. "We also didn't know how many people's lives we might endanger by stopping the trains. Just imagine! What if the robbers realized we were on to them, and took hostages?"

Just then Looey's mobile rang.

ÜBUNG 60

Übung 60: Sind die folgenden Wörter in britischer und/oder amerikanischer Weise buchstabiert?

1. analyze ______________________
2. prioritize ______________________
3. categorise ______________________
4. criticize ______________________
5. homogenize ______________________
6. memorize ______________________
7. recognise ______________________

"LaCapra." She listened.

"Right, *Boss,*" she said, and rang off.

"Agent O'Leary wants us back at headquarters on the double. They found another piece of that corpse. At least, we assume it's the same corpse. I'm going to have to call someone else to continue your tour of our fair *subway* system. Excuse me, please."

Looey hit her speed dial.

"Hello, Carolyn? This is Looey. We've got an emergency at the task force. Right, you guessed it. I hear you're on duty as backup from the MTA. Could you report to Operation Skyline as soon as you can? I need someone to show a detective around the *subway*."

Looey and Hudson mounted the stairs.

"That's the first time I've heard you address another police *officer* by name," remarked Inspector Hudson, remembering their earlier conversation about rank.

"You caught me there, sir," smiled Looey. "Carolyn is officially a *patrol officer* of the Metropolitan Transit Authority – but she's also my sister."

Übung 61: Setzen Sie die Kurzformen ein!

Back at headquarters, they were greeted by O'Leary, who asked, "(1. Can you not) __________ go out to breakfast without coming back with a corpse?"

"(2. They are) __________ out there, sir," said Looey seriously.

Sergeant Ozbek piped up from his desk. "Spoken like a true police *officer.*"

"And besides, this (3. one is) __________ only part of a corpse."

"(4. That is) __________ our lieutenant," said Ozbek.

"(5. Let us) __________ be serious. I called you back because the MTA *just turned up* (has just turned up) a missing piece of the puzzle, in the subway station at 14th Street Union Square," said O'Leary. "Specifically, it appears to be another piece of the poor soul whose leg was found in Grand Central this morning."

"Any idea who it is?"

"No. But James, this brings us back to the question you asked when you arrived yesterday: How will we know (6. there is) __________ a power struggle going on in the Skyline Syndicate?"

O'Leary ran his hands over his face.

"(7. We will) ______________ know it when the bodies start washing up."

Peter Stanley walked in the door, whistling.

"A man with a clear conscience," observed Sergeant Ozbek. "A man who does not check his email on the way to work."

"Did I miss something here?" Stanley looked around. "Blimey! *(I'll be darned!)* Did you catch Fat Frankie?"

"We've got somebody," said Ozbek. "We just don't know who."

"Well, do we know who did it?" asked Stanley, optimistically.

"Yes," stated Sergeant Jones. "Every *nut* who called in between midnight and six this morning."

Hudson looked over to where Jones had been sitting by the phone all night, and thought: "Seems over six feet even seated, muscular build, kinky brown hair, brown eyes, black *(African-American),* very dark complexion, male."

"Why are we not getting any information?" wondered O'Leary. "Nothing rational on the phone line. Nothing from the usual set of songbirds. Nothing at all." O'Leary shoved his hands in his pockets.

"Dead silence! Usually there are ten guys awaiting trial who can't wait to sell their brother down the river on the chance it will lower their jail term."

Hudson remembered what the cab driver had said.

"Maybe they're afraid, Gene."

"These guys do not know the meaning of the word, James. They just want to get out of jail."

"Maybe they don't want to wind up like Charlie."

"Charlie?"

"That chap ((guy)) in Grand Central," said Hudson. "He deserves a name. 'Charlie' will do, at least until we find out who he really was."

"It's very strange, James, all the same. I've never heard such deafening silence."

Übung 62: Verbinden Sie die passenden Satzteile!

1. "Why not?"	☐	he yelled.
2. "You win,"	☐	she commanded.
3. "Let's go,"	☐	she mused.
4. "Hands up!"	☐	she hissed.
5. "I wonder …"	☐	she urged.
6. "Go away!"	☐	he wondered.
7. "Selfish snake!"	☐	he conceded.

Hudson walked over to where Looey had spread out some maps of the city on her desk.

"The first leg was found in Grand Central. The MTA found the second leg in the 14th Street-Union Square Station," she said. "Why were both body parts found in train stations?"

"Maybe it's a coincidence?" quipped Ozbek, from the next desk.

"Or simple stupidity," answered Looey. "Whoever put Charlie in the stations might have thought the pieces would never be found."

"The work of a genius," continued Ozbek. "I'm putting my money on Salvatore del Monaco."

"After all," said Looey, ignoring Ozbek, "each piece was carefully sealed in a black plastic *garbage bag* before being dumped in yet another bag."

"I've been thinking about that myself," mused Hudson. "What motivated the cleaning woman in Grand Central to open the bag?"

"She didn't," said Looey. "That much Spanish I can understand. The body bag was already open when she went to *dump the trash* (put out the rubbish). In fact, it was opened in such a way that she had to see the leg."

"What if the bag had been opened by someone who was merely looking for empty bottles or cans to return?" asked Hudson.

"That would make sense. He must have got the shock of his life, and run out the door, leaving the bag wide open."

"If it were a homeless person, that would go a long way to explain why he did not report what he had seen. No matter who it was, though, a lot of people seem to know they would live longer if they keep quiet about the recent criminal activity," said Hudson.

"No one wants to find themselves on the wrong side of the Skyline Syndicate," agreed Looey.

"We must keep an open mind, however," urged Hudson. "What if the murderer intended for someone to find and report the body parts? Perhaps it was meant to be a message."

"Do you think the Skyline Syndicate wanted to threaten people who might consider helping us with information about the robbery? Maybe they thought that displaying a dead body would give people the idea that they, too, might be killed?"

"I'm thinking …" said Hudson. "Actually, I'm thinking that it is the placement of the pieces of Charlie's body, as well as the body itself, that is the message. But I don't know yet what precisely is significant about the fact that both pieces were left in train stations."

ÜBUNG 63 !

Übung 63: Ordnen Sie die folgenden Sätze in der Reihenfolge eines sinnvollen Telefongesprächs!

1. May I leave a message?
2. My name is Mrs Newbury.
3. May I speak to Mr White?
4. Hello.
5. I'm calling on behalf of Wadgeley College.
6. Good morning.

7. Yes, of course.
8. He's not in at the moment.

Lösung: _ _ _ _ _ _ _ _ _ _

"I was just looking at maps of the *subway* system," said Looey. "There is something that Union Square has in common with Grand Central. They are both stations where a large number of lines cross." She pointed to a list: "F, V, L, 1, 2, 3, 9."

"That is even more lines than we walked through this morning," said Hudson, surprised.

"You can even catch two separate PATH trains at Union Square," said Looey. "Those are commuter trains that run to New Jersey. That's something else the stations have in common: commuter trains from both stations will take you right out of the city."

Looey shuffled the maps to find one that showed a larger view of the *subway* system.

"New Jersey is really no farther away than Long Island – even Queens is already Long Island, technically speaking. But they all seem very far away from us here in midtown Manhattan," she continued. "We've got enough on our hands with the local *subways.* See here, at Union Square? Some of those *subway* lines run crosstown, and some of them run uptown and downtown," she said.

"That is something else that Grand Central and Union Square stations have in common. They are crossroads," observed Hudson.

"Eerie, isn't it? I wonder …"

"I never really thought of it that way," admitted Looey. "I'm usually too busy catching my train."

"It used to be," said Hudson quietly, "that suicides were buried at the crossroads. They were considered outcasts, and were not allowed to be buried with the community. Maybe someone wanted to send the message that Charlie had in some way committed suicide, or was cast out by his community."

"Because he had betrayed the Syndicate?"

"Perhaps he did not betray the Syndicate to the outside," mused Hudson. "Perhaps he in some sense committed suicide by making trouble within the Syndicate itself. What if he crossed Fat Frankie? As Agent O'Leary said, we know when there's trouble within the Syndicate – when the bodies start washing up."

ÜBUNG 64 !

Übung 64: Unterstreichen Sie im nächsten Abschnitt die sechs Wörter, die auf ***-ing*** *enden! Welches der Wörter passt nicht zu den anderen Wörtern?* ____________________

"*Boss*, I just took a very strange call," said Sergeant Jones to Lieutenant LaCapra. "I think you ought to listen to this."

Sergeant Jones put the phone on speaker and hit the replay button. A young woman spoke. She was clearly struggling to remain in control of her voice.

"I don't know whether this has anything to do with that cop who was shot," she said. "But I was just walking along the East River with my son. He's three years old. I made him look up into the tree to see if he could find a bird, because I didn't want him to see what was floating down the river … "

"Yes, ma'am, I'm listening," said Sergeant Jones on the recording.

"It was an arm."

"Can you tell us, ma'am, exactly where you were when you saw it?"

A click was heard on the recording. She was gone.

“Have you got a tracer on that call?” asked Looey.
“It came from downtown,” said Jones. “Near Alphabet City.”

“That’s downriver from Union Square,” Looey explained to Hudson. “It’s Fat Frankie’s territory.”
“Do you want me to alert the precincts, Looey?”
“Please do, Jones. Alert everybody downstream, and I mean all the way out to Gravesend Bay. I want that arm.”
She looked at Inspector Hudson. “Where there’s an arm, there’s a hand,” she said.
Hudson completed her thought. “And where there’s a hand, there are fingerprints.”

Übung 65: Bringen Sie jeden der Sätze in die richtige Reihenfolge!

(1. Stanley/called/Chief/to/the/them/room/across/.)

“I think I’ve got something here,” he said. “Would you have a butcher’s ((take a look)), Inspector Hudson?”

Stanley had displayed what looked like bank records on his computer screen.

“This is a list of bank accounts in the name of Sylvia Leporello. (2. wife/Frankie/Fat/’s/is/she/.)”

(3. the/Looey/stared/Hudson/at/and/screen/.)

"She sure has a lot of bank accounts," said Looey.

(4. money/also/got/she's/lot/a/of/.)"

"Some of the accounts have a lot of money in them," agreed Stanley. "But that's not the surprising part. Look more closely at these entries." He tapped on his keyboard, and several of the entries showed up in greater detail.

"I don't understand," said Looey. "Some of those accounts only have a hundred dollars in them."

"And they've all been opened in the last month," added Stanley.

(5. looked/pleased/he/himself/very/with/.)

(6. the/in/O'Leary/doorway/appeared/agent/.)

"It's not often that *Mr.* (Mr) Paperwork gets so much attention," he remarked. "What's up?"

"Fat Frankie's wife – whether she knows it or not – is the proud owner of eleven brand-new bank accounts," announced Stanley. "She's gormless ((clueless)), if you ask me. But I'd say that someone has been getting ready to transfer a whole lot of money out of New York."

"A million and a half dollars, maybe?" asked O'Leary. "Well, the money from the bank robbery yesterday has to go somewhere. Good work, Peter."

Agent O'Leary turned to Lieutenant LaCapra. "I want you to get together a list of anyone who might be able to give us inside information about what Fat Frankie is up to. We especially want to know what the connection might be between Fat Frankie and the body parts that have been found. Put the word out that we are ready to deal."

Hudson was next on O'Leary's list.

"James, I hear you have an appointment with an MTA *officer* to tour the largest *subway* station in New York City. And when you've seen enough of the underbelly of Times Square, I suggest the two of you take a quick trip down to Union Square."

"But first," O'Leary said, "it's lunchtime."

*Übung 66: Verbinden Sie die **if-Sätze** mit dem passenden zweiten Satzteil!*

ÜBUNG 66 !

1. If it's noon,	☐ let's eat lunch!
2. If he crosses Frankie,	☐ please call.
3. If I had seen you,	☐ Frankie will kill him.
4. If you see her,	☐ you'll get to Times Square.
5. If you go,	☐ I would have said hello.
6. If she's right,	☐ I'll go, too.
7. If you take the shuttle,	☐ he's wrong.

Sergeant Ozbek opened his desk drawer and brought out a stack of menus. "We usually order *take-out* (take-away) from one of the restaurants downstairs," he told Inspector Hudson. "The food will be here in no time."

"I'll have a hamburger and *French fries* (chips)," said Looey Looey. "And a Coke."

"I'll have a pastrami sandwich on rye bread," said Stanley.

"What would you like, Inspector?"

"Perhaps I will have … a chicken wrap," said Inspector Hudson. "With chips, please. And another cup of Earl Grey tea."

"Would you prefer something hot to eat, after your long trip, sir? I know it's dinner time in London."

"I can hardly think about eating," said Inspector Hudson.

"Jones usually brings food from home," said Ozbek, glancing in Jones' direction.

"That was before the *Boss* asked me to work a double shift," said Jones. "I'll have what the Inspector is having."

Ozbek rolled his eyes, pressed the speed dial and ordered, adding a hamburger for himself. In minutes, the desk sergeant from the reception appeared at their door with the bag of food.

Hudson could hardly follow the conversation. He ate only half the chicken wrap.

ÜBUNG 67 !

Übung 67: Bestellen Sie das Mittagsessen! Unterstreichen Sie die Sätze, die keine Fehler enthalten, und verbessern Sie die Fehler!

1. Pastrami on rye, please. ____________

2. I'll have the daily special. ____________

3. Three chicken wrap and three cola. ____________

4. How soon could you deliver a mushroom pizza? ____________

5. Two hamburgers to go, please. ____________

6. A chicken salads sandwich, please. ____________

7. Tofu and vegetables under rice, please. ____________

Patrol Officer Carolyn LaCapra of the Metropolitan Transit Authority reported for duty as the members of the task force were tipping the rubbish *(throwing out the garbage).*
"I want you to stay in close touch," warned Looey. "And I do not want anything to happen to the Inspector here."
Patrol Officer LaCapra thought to herself that Inspector Hudson looked like his biggest problem would be getting lost on the *subway.* "Yes, *Boss*," she said, and they walked out the door.
The phone rang on Sergeant Jones' desk. He waved over to Looey and put the phone on speaker. Looey gestured for the room to be quiet.
"My boy is a good boy," sobbed the woman on the other end of the line. "He didn't want to rob that *liquor* store. It's those bad boys he hangs out with, and those older men I told you about."
"Yes, ma'am," said Sergeant Jones, nodding.
"You talk to him," said his mother. "He'll tell you."
"Thank you very much, ma'am. We have your number, and remember, you can call us any time."
Sergeant Jones rang off.

ÜBUNG 68 !

Übung 68: Tragen Sie die Komparative und Superlative ein!

1. ripe ____________

2. big ____________

3. bad ______

4. old ______

5. small ______

6. extreme ______

7. far ______

8. pretty ______

"Her son just got arrested. He's mixed up with some bad company, and he heard them talking about the murder."

"Ozbek, find out who's on duty downtown where they're holding that young man. Ask if there's a female detective. I want this handled with extreme care."

"Right, *Boss*."

"And you might as well start making arrangements with the Witness Protection Program."

Looey sighed as she thought of the young man. It might be just as well that he start another life.

"When you're through with that, I want both of you – Jones and Ozbek – to go home and get some sleep," said O'Leary. "I need you both back on duty later tonight."

Looey drummed her fingers on her desk. It looked like Sal del Monaco and Fat Frankie were fighting one another for control of the Skyline Syndicate. There wasn't enough information yet to identify the corpse, but it might already be Sal. Perhaps it wasn't too soon to call Frankie in for questioning. She decided to wait for the coroner's report, and for whatever the young *liquor* store artist had to say. Looey picked up a pen and started filling out paperwork to request that Fat Frankie be called in for questioning in the death of the unidentified person known as Charlie.

Übung 69: Am Telefon – kreuzen Sie die im vorgegebenen Zusammenhang richtige Aussage an!

1. Good morning.
a) ☒ My name is Professor Sturges.
b) ☐ Who's this?

2. I'm calling on behalf of the Boffo Company.
a) ☒ Is Ms Jefferson in?
b) ☐ Put Mr Wesley on the line straightaway.

3. Hello. This is Mrs Weatherall.
a) ☐ What time is it, please?
b) ☒ May I speak to your mother, please?

4. Good morning. I am calling on behalf of Dr Smith.
a) ☒ Am I inopportune?
b) ☐ Do you know why I am calling?

5. Good evening. Fraser here.
a) ☒ Do you have a moment to discuss the Bliffen case?
b) ☐ Why are you calling me?

"Lieutenant LaCapra, ma'am?"
Looey Looey started out of a sound sleep. "What is it Sergeant?"
"There's a Detective Chen here to see you, from downtown."
Looey groaned. "Guess I fell asleep there. Send her in. Better yet, ask Agent O'Leary if he would like to be present."
They met in Agent O'Leary's office. Detective Chen took out several sheets of paper and said, "I just met with Izzy Washington, the young man Lieutenant LaCapra called about earlier. This is a sworn statement provided by *Mr.* (Mr) Washington."

"Thank you very much, Detective," said O'Leary. "We appreciate your coming all the way up here."
"I am aware of the seriousness of *Mr.* Washington's situation," said Detective Chen. "I am afraid that he is not."
"What did he have to say?" asked O'Leary.
"He is convinced that nothing can go wrong for him, because he is under the protection of Fat Frankie."
"He said this in so many words?"
"He bragged about it. He told me that Fat Frankie was out to 'annihilate the competition', in *Mr.* Washington's words. He repeats this phrase like a broken record. We don't have the drug tests on him back yet, but he sounds like he's either on drugs or brainwashed."
"Does he know anything about those body parts?" asked O'Leary.
"He's not too coherent, Agent O'Leary – just convinced."

! ÜBUNG 70

Übung 70: Was sind die Familienwurzeln dieser Amerikanerinnen und Amerikaner?

1. Detective Chen	5	Turkish
2. Lieutenant LaCapra	2	Italian
3. Agent O'Leary	1	Chinese
4. Sergeant Jones	6	Indian
5. Sergeant Ozbek	3	Irish
6. Arjun Patel	4	African-American

"Is he a reliable source?"
"He's telling the truth as he sees it, I believe. I picked up a few details by listening to him go over and over the same point," said Detective Chen.
"What point?" asked Looey.

"'Annihilation of the competition'," said Chen.
O'Leary sighed.
"What makes his account plausible is that there would be no reason to invent the details. More importantly, I don't think a person with any experience would have chosen to tell us these things. He has put himself in great danger, and he doesn't even realize it."
"What did he bargain for?"
"Nothing," said Chen. "He is convinced that Fat Frankie is going to swoop in and save him."
"Did you hear anything that would confirm that Fat Frankie is involved in the murder this morning?"
There was a knock at the door.
"I'm sorry to disturb you," said the sergeant, "but the coroner's report just arrived."
The sergeant handed O'Leary a fax.
O'Leary scanned the report and then read aloud.
"'The subject appears to weigh 250 pounds or more.'"
"Wow," said Looey, quietly. "Frankie was involved, alright."

Übung 71: Bringen Sie den Dialog in die richtige Reihenfolge!

1. You don't say!
2. Who is it?
3. Did you see the news this morning?
4. What's more, the police have found the killer!
5. No. What happened?
6. Mr Sparks has been murdered!

Lösung: _ _ _ _ _ _

"Izzy Washington is right about one thing," said O'Leary. "It seems that someone in the Skyline Syndicate is out to annihilate the competition. Unfortunately, *Mr.* Washington did not pick the winner."

"Neither did we, *Boss,*" said Looey.

Agent O'Leary glared at her.

"With all due respect, *Boss*."

"Thank you very much for your visit, Detective Chen," said Agent O'Leary. "We'd better get back to work. Let me know if you need my help on the Washington case."

James Hudson and Carolyn LaCapra arrived back at the task force headquarters looking a bit worn out.

"How was Times Square, 'Crossroads of the World'?" asked Looey.

"There were millions of people, as usual," said LaCapra. "Most of them were minding their own business."

"There were huge video projections on the buildings around Times Square," said Inspector Hudson.

"And *patrol officers* handing out flyers in front of every *theater* (theatre) and on every street corner," added LaCapra.

"We saw the ticket office right in the middle of the theatre district. The news ticker running right around the corner of a building tells everyone in Times Square what's happening everywhere on earth," marvelled *(marveled)* Hudson.

"The news ticker asks people to call us with information about the robbery or *Officer* Mahoney," said LaCapra.

"We saw the lights of Broadway," said Hudson. "Many lights are on even in the afternoon, you know. I'll never forget it."

"It's a little more impressive at night, sir."

"I tried to get him to walk over to Radio City Music Hall to see the Rockettes, but he wasn't interested," said LaCapra.

Übung 72: Geben Sie zu folgenden Wörtern die amerikanische Schreibweise an!

1. theatre ______________________
2. criticise ______________________
3. realise ______________________
4. analyse ______________________
5. deputise ______________________
6. practise ______________________
7. water ______________________

"We walked through what seemed like miles of Underground," sighed Hudson. "It seems that half the life of New York is lived underground."

"It is," said Looey. "And it's our job to police it. Look here. I took a *subway* map and marked every line that passes through Grand Central or Times Square."

Looey tacked the map up on the wall so everyone could see.

"I almost forgot," she said. "Did you get to Union Square?"

"They still had the crime scene taped off," replied LaCapra. "We looked around, but I'm afraid nothing came to mind," said Hudson.

"Here, look at this." Looey pointed to the map. "Remember when we were over at the Transatlantic Bank, and we discussed the *subway* lines that lead away from the scene of the crime?"

"I noted that there were so many *subway* lines, there were more than enough lines for each of the three robbers."

"You said that if they were smart, they would split up," said Looey. "Based on your idea, I worked up a possible scenario."
She picked up a black biro *(ballpoint pen)*.

ÜBUNG 73 !

*Übung 73: Unterstreichen Sie die verschiedenen **Richtungen,** in die die drei Räuber geflohen sein könnten! Markieren Sie die Richtungen mit 1, 2 und 3!*

"Let's say the three robbers split up and each took a different getaway train. One might have taken a 4, 5 or 6 train on the green line that goes downtown, here. One might have taken the 7 train west, which is this purple line, here, one stop to Times Square. The third robber? Let's say he took the shuttle to Times Square."

Looey had drawn three lines. One went downtown, and two went west to Times Square.
"Now let's just say that the two who went to Times Square changed trains. They would not really be anywhere near one another, because as you experienced today, that station is enormous. Let's say that Robber Number Two changed from the 7 train to the very next train that came in on the red line – any train at all. There are four: 1, 2, 3 or 9. He would have been out of there in a heartbeat, headed downtown."
She drew another fat black line going downtown. So far, she had the top and two sides of a square. The two top corners were Grand Central Station at the right and Times Square at the left. Two of the robbers were now travelling downtown.
"Robber Number Three gets off the shuttle at Times Square and changes for any of the four trains going downtown on the yellow line: the N, Q, R or W trains. He too would be gone in a flash."

Übung 74: Geben Sie zu folgenden Wörtern die amerikanische Schreibweise an!

1. travelling ______________________
2. fulfil ______________________
3. skilful ______________________
4. jewellery ______________________
5. draught ______________________
6. plough ______________________

Looey drew a third fat black line from Times Square going downtown. This line ran diagonally down from the top left corner.

Her diagram showed Robbers One and Two meeting up only four stops later.

"That's Union Square," said LaCapra.

"Thank you, Miss *Subways*," said Looey. "Inspector, would you like to connect the dots?"

Inspector Hudson took the pen.

"Robber Number Three," he said, "would have to change trains one more time. He would transfer to the L train. In two stops, he too would be in Union Square."

The square was now complete, with a diagonal line running from the top left corner to the lower right corner.

"They set out on different trains," Looey said, "and end up in the same place."

"It does start to look as if Union Square is a hot spot."

"Well, and there's Charlie," added LaCapra.

"I meant to tell you," said Looey suddenly, "about Charlie."

Übung 75: Ordnen Sie zu!

1. The robbers begin	3	to Times Square.
2. One travels directly	5	at Union Square.
3. Two first go	1	near Grand Central Station.
4. Two of them must	4	change trains.
5. All three meet again	2	downtown.
6. They start in	7	together.
7. But they wind up	6	different directions.

"It's not official yet," said Looey. "But there's every reason to believe that Charlie is Frankie."

"Whoa, back up!" cried *Patrol Officer* LaCapra.

"You'd better sit down for this one," said Looey. She explained about Detective Chen's visit, Izzy Washington's story, and the coroner's report.

"Well, here we are," said Hudson. "We don't know who robbed the bank and shot Mahoney. We don't know who killed Frankie, either. And we don't know who is the new leader of the Skyline Syndicate."

"If you'll excuse me," said *Patrol Officer* LaCapra, "I have to get back to Grand Central."

Her big sister glared at her.

"Big help you are!"

Patrol Officer LaCapra waved goodbye.

"Perhaps while we are waiting for inspiration," said Inspector Hudson, "we might review the video of the robbery. Sir Reginald showed me the clip you put on the internet before I left London. I watched it many times on the aeroplane, as well. One never knows."

The two of them headed for O'Leary's office.

"I hope he's not sleeping," said Looey. "O'Leary hasn't left his office since the robbery occurred. He's a pretty dedicated guy." She knocked softly on the door.
"Come in."
"Excuse me, *Boss*. I was wondering if Inspector Hudson and I could watch the video of the bank robbery."
"*Sure thing* ((Certainly)), Looey. Do you mind if I join you?"
"We could use some fresh ideas, *Boss*," said Looey.
Agent O'Leary handed the remote control to Lieutenant LaCapra. The video began to play.

! ÜBUNG 76

Übung 76: Setzen Sie die richtige Ortsangabe ein! Es sind gegebenenfalls auch mehrere Alternativen richtig.
(as far as, near, bottom, up, into, out of, edge)

The camera was located in the lobby of the Transatlantic Bank, 1. __________ the ceiling. It recorded everyone who came 2. __________ the front door. A bit of the pavement could be seen, 3. __________ the kerb. At the 4. __________ of the picture, an armoured car pulled 5. __________. One could see the 6. __________ of a door opening, and a man's legs as he got out of the armoured car.

The three investigators watched as a uniformed security guard approached the door holding a large bag.
The glass door to the bank opened.
"Here he comes," said LaCapra. "And here come the bad guys."

Three men ran up to the guard's left side as he was opening the door. The men wore women's nylon stockings pulled over their heads. All three had guns.

One man held his gun by the barrel. He swung it from above down against the guard's temple. The guard crumpled to the floor.

The three robbers stuffed the bags of money into backpacks.

LaCapra turned to Inspector Hudson. "Why is it that your police *officers* don't carry – "

"Looey!" said Agent O'Leary sharply. "I told you we would not discuss firearms."

"Yes, *Boss,*" said Looey.

One of the robbers looked up and down the avenue as the other two finished stuffing their backpacks. The first robber froze, crouched, and, holding his gun with both hands, fired.

All three ran out of the frame.

"Could we see that again, please?" asked Inspector Hudson.

Looey rewound the video.

The robbers disappeared out of the frame, and the security guard walked quickly backwards. The episode started again. The guard walked toward the door.

"Could you play this bit ((part)) in slow motion?"

Inspector Hudson seemed suddenly agitated.

In slow motion, the first robber took the last step toward the guard. He led with his left foot. He rose up, with his weight on his left foot, raising his right arm at the same time. As he rose up, he drew his right foot forward until it almost met his left foot. Then he struck. As his body weight came down, his right foot slid back again, the right knee bending deeply to absorb the shock.

"This guy could have been a ballerina," said Looey.

"It's Michael Masterson," said Inspector Hudson quietly.

"Who?" asked Agent O'Leary and Looey in unison. "You know this guy?"
"All too well," said Inspector Hudson. "Look at the way he moves. This man knows how to use his whole body – and with deadly force. Most men just stand there and swing."

Übung 77: Stellen Sie die richtigen Wörter über Bewegungsabläufe zusammen!

1. slow	☐	time
2. rose	☐	hard
3. deadly	1	motion
4. bending	2	up
5. struck	☐	deeply
6. same	☐	force

"How do you know him?" asked O'Leary.
"He's on Scotland Yard's Most Wanted list."
Agent O'Leary stepped to the other side of his desk and called up ((brought up)) the website of Scotland Yard.
"Him?" asked O'Leary.
Hudson stared at a familiar photograph and read the story he knew all too well:

"We are appealing for information about the whereabouts of 36-year-old Michael Masterson, a convicted murderer and armed robber.
Masterson escaped from prison, where he was serving a life sentence, having been convicted of murder, armed robbery and firearm offences."

"Masterson shot a police constable," said Inspector Hudson. Hudson's eyes fell once again to the words on the Most Wanted website:

"Police Constable Richard Conroy was shot in the chest as he attempted to intervene. PC Conroy died of his injuries and was posthumously awarded the Queen's Gallantry Medal for his bravery."

! ÜBUNG 78

Übung 78: Sind die folgenden Sätze richtig oder falsch? Markieren Sie mit richtig ✔ oder falsch –!

1. Police Constable Conroy captured Masterson. ☐
2. Michael Masterson was on the FBI's Most Wanted List. ☐
3. The robber is familiar with firearms. ☐
4. Masterson stabbed the constable. ☐
5. Inspector Hudson knows Masterson's whereabouts. ☐
6. Deadly force is easy to achieve. ☐

"I remember the trial," said Inspector Hudson, grimly. "Masterson showed no remorse."
Hudson sighed and continued. "I remember the day he escaped from prison, too. Masterson struck a prison guard, and the poor guard almost died. He was struck with a knife from above, between the neck and shoulder."
"But that was a knife, sir," said Looey.
"It is the body movement that is remarkably similar," said Hudson. "Masterson's attack was caught on videotape by a surveillance camera in the prison. The technique is very similar to what we have just seen in the video taken in New York. You might ring up Sir

Reginald and ask for a copy of the video that is on file at Scotland Yard. You can compare them yourselves."

"It's a pretty distinctive way of striking," said Agent O'Leary. "I will call Sir Reginald for the tape, but I think we can take your word for it for now."

"Masterson is a dangerous man," said Hudson. "And if he is involved in the struggle for control of the Skyline Syndicate, we are in big trouble."

"We're in trouble, alright," said O'Leary. "And I'm very grateful that we have you working with us on this case. Now at least we know who it is we're looking for. With your experience, we stand a chance at catching Masterson, and bringing down the Skyline Syndicate."

"Are you alright, sir?" asked Looey. "You look a bit pale."

"It's very bad news," said Hudson. "And I must admit, I suddenly feel a bit ill."

Übung 79: Ordnen Sie den Fragen die richtigen Antworten zu!

1. How are you today?	[4] I was, but I'm better now.
2. How is your wife?	[5] My temperature is 100.2.
3. What did the doctor say?	[2] She is very well, thank you.
4. Is it true you were ill?	[1] Fine, thank you.
5. Do you have a fever?	[3] He recommended bed rest.

Agent O'Leary looked at his watch. "It's jet lag, James. It might be time for you to head back to the Ivy Club. We can't afford to have you get sick."

"If only I had watched the entire video before this!" lamented Inspector Hudson.

"That can't be helped," said O'Leary.
"We had a few other things to do besides watch videos!" exclaimed Looey. "And you've only been here for one day!"
"We sent Scotland Yard the video clip we thought was the heart of the matter," said O'Leary. "And we would never post on the internet the video of the actual attack. We must think of the security guard's privacy."
"If only I had – "
"Please, James. You need rest. I'm going to ask one of the *officers* to escort you back to your room. Thanks to you, we have something to go on. You can be sure that we will initiate a full-scale search."
Back at the Ivy Club, Hudson ordered dinner from room service and fell into bed.

ÜBUNG 80 !

Übung 80: Vervollständigen Sie die Sätze mit passenden Verben! Achten Sie dabei auf die richtige Zeitform!

1. We would never ________________ that video on the internet.
2. If only Hudson had ____________ the whole video!
3. Looey ____________ the video.
4. The attack was ________________ on videotape.
5. The attack was ________________.
6. One can ______________ or buy videos.

Inspector Hudson woke up in a sweat in a totally dark room.
"It's just a nightmare," he thought. But then he remembered it was all too real. Michael Masterson had struck again, and was on his way to taking over the biggest crime syndicate in New York.

The clock said it was four in the morning. Hudson dragged himself out of bed and headed for the task force headquarters.
The headquarters looked different this morning. The first thing Hudson saw was Michael Masterson's face, looking out from posters that had been printed from the Scotland Yard Most Wanted website. Stacks of flyers appealing for information about Masterson lay on the tables. The walls were covered with detailed information about Michael Masterson. His appearance, his habits, his behaviour *(behavior)* – everything that was known about Masterson was posted on the walls.
"It's looking a bit like Scotland Yard in here," remarked Hudson.
"Good morning, sir," said Jones and Ozbek, in a chorus.
"You don't even have to ask, sir," continued Ozbek. "Every cop in the city has Masterson's face memorized (memorised). Every news show on the radio and television stations has carried the announcement. We even woke up Sir Reginald to get him to record a thirty-second spot for the eleven o'clock news."
"Sir Reginald?" exclaimed Inspector Hudson. "He can't have been pleased."
"He was thrilled, sir," said Ozbek. "Just imagine! If we catch Masterson, we will have caught the main bank robber, the likely leader of the Skyline Syndicate, and a man who's on the Most Wanted List of Scotland Yard." Ozbek ticked off the items on his fingers.
"He's wanted as a cop-killer in two countries," added Jones. "We'll get him, sir."

Übung 81: Unterstreichen Sie jeweils die stärkere Emotion!

1. I was pleased/thrilled.
2. She was disappointed/crushed.

3. He was happy/ecstatic.
4. He was furious/angry.
5. They were hungry/starved.
6. I was sad/depressed.

Hudson noticed that there were now packets of Earl Grey tea next to the coffee machine. He stepped over to pour himself some hot water.

"Don't tell me you're all up already," Hudson said to Looey.

"So are you, I see, sir. How's the jet lag this morning?"

Looey was studying the *subway* map.

"Remember the lines we discussed yesterday?" asked Looey. "Look what happens when I follow them farther downtown."

Hudson looked at the lines that Looey had drawn on the map.

"They cross again, sir, at Fulton Street."

Hudson and Looey stared at the tangle of lines that made up the Fulton Street station. Four north-south and east-west lines met in a crossroads.

"That looks almost as big as Times Square," remarked Hudson. "What's down there?"

Looey pointed to two separate stations with the same name, one stop down from Fulton Street. They were both called "Wall Street."

"The financial district, sir."

"Oh, no," said Hudson. "Oh, no."

Looey's phone rang.

"It's Manhattan South," she yelled. "There's a bank robbery in progress! Three men have knocked a security guard unconscious. They are making off with the cash that was meant for the ATM machines at the Fulton Street Shipping Bank!"

Looey and Hudson turned back immediately to the *subway* map.

"We could stop a train," said Looey. "But which one? If they're

headed back to Fourteenth Street, they could take any one of seven trains! There are four trains on the red line – 1,2,3 and 9 – and three on the green line – 4,5,6. We can't stop seven trains!"
"What we need," said Hudson, "is one more piece of information. If we had just one more coordinate on the map!"

Übung 82: Welches Wort passt nicht in die Wortreihe? Unterstreichen Sie das schwarze Schaf!

ÜBUNG 82 !

1. quick, hasty, pace, slow, hurry
2. raining, breezy, pouring, sleeting, snowing
3. roaches, rats, mice, crocodiles, ants
4. Piccadilly Circus, Fulton Street, Times Square, Grand Central, Union Square
5. Wall Street, midtown, Stock Exchange, downtown, financial district
6. stable, strong, powerful, mighty, influential

They were interrupted by the powerful voice of Sergeant Jones, who was about to lose his temper.
"We have a bank robbery in progress!" he yelled into the telephone receiver. "If you have cockroaches, call the Board of Health! We have no inspectors here!"
Inspector Hudson shouted, "Wait! Don't hang up on that man! I am Inspector Hudson!"
He grabbed the telephone receiver.
"Inspector Hudson here!" he shouted.
"Okay, okay," said the man on the other end. "This is Arjun Patel. I'm the cab driver who took you from the airport to the Ivy Club the other day. Remember me?"

"I do indeed," said Hudson. "But I am in rather a dreadful hurry at the moment. There is a bank robbery in progress."
"That's what I'm calling about," said Patel. "I'm calling to tell you that, well …"
"Quick, man! Out with it! Please!" cried Hudson.
Patel took a deep breath.
"The morning of the robbery, before the news was out, I picked up a guy at Union Square. He looked like he had just run a mile. He was carrying a big backpack. When I first heard the Police Commissioner on the radio ask for information about someone who had robbed a bank and shot a cop, I was too afraid to call in. But after I talked to you – "
"Where did you take him?" shouted Hudson.
"Brooklyn, sir. I took him to a house near Court Street."
Hudson shouted into the room.
"This is an emergency! Masterson is based in Brooklyn! Looey, look at the map!"

ÜBUNG 83 !

Übung 83: Setzen Sie die richtigen Wörter in die Leerstellen ein!

"It's Court Street, sir! I can't believe it! The red and green lines meet again just across the river in

1. ______________________! The next crossroads is Court Street, indeed!"

"Get the MTA!" shouted Hudson. "Stop the 2. ______________ that is on its way right now from Fulton Street to

3. ______________________!"

"Thank you, Patel," said Hudson into the telephone. "Thank you very much. Please stay on the line."

Hudson handed the 4. ______________________ to Sergeant Jones.

"Keep this man on the 5. __________," he said sharply.

"It's dead, *Boss*," said the sergeant. "He *hung* 6. __________. He must have been scared."

"Looey, it's the train to Brooklyn," cried Hudson. But she was already running to Agent 7. __________ office, where Chief Daniels of the MTA was taking a turn sleeping on O'Leary's couch.

In seconds, Chief Daniels ran into the headquarters. He was already on his mobile, being transferred to the driver of the train. The train had just begun its long trip through the tunnel under the water between Manhattan and Brooklyn.

"We've got a chance, sir," said Looey to Inspector Hudson. "The trip between Fulton Street and Court Street is very long. It might be the longest ride between two *subway* stops in the whole city."

"This is Chief Daniels of the MTA," said the chief to the driver. "This is an emergency."

"What do you mean by 'long'?" asked Hudson.

"Oh, maybe seven minutes," said Looey.

Hudson felt his heart race.

"Do not stop the train," said Daniels. "I repeat, this is an emergency. Do not stop the train. Please remain calm. I want you to slow the train down – very slowly, driver. Do you understand me? Do not alarm the passengers. Very slowly."

"Slow the train down," repeated the driver. "Roger, Chief Daniels. Very slowly. What's happening, Chief?"

"Very slowly, driver," said Chief Daniels. "I want you to delay the arrival of the train into Court Street. Do not stop the train. What is your position and speed, driver?"

"I just entered (I've just entered) the tunnel," said the driver. "I am now proceeding at five miles an hour. Four. Three. Two. What's the matter?"

"It's alright, driver. You are not in danger. Please remain calm. There are three bank robbers on your train. They are armed and dangerous. We want to avoid panic among the passengers."

"My train is almost empty, sir," said the driver. "I checked the mirrors before I closed the doors at Fulton Street."

Chief Daniels finally breathed.

ÜBUNG 84 !

Übung 84: Setzen Sie die Sätze in die direkte Rede!

1. Looey said that the trip takes seven minutes.

____

2. Patel told Hudson that he took the man to Brooklyn.

____

3. The driver asked what was wrong.

____

4. Looey said that they might have enough time.

____

5. Chief Daniels told the driver not to stop the train.

6. Looey hoped he wasn't sleeping.

7. Patel said that on the morning of the robbery, before the news was out, he had picked up a guy at Union Square.

"I want you to keep those doors locked, driver," said Chief Daniels. "Slow that train down to a crawl. We need every second you can give us to evacuate the platform at Court Street."

"Roger, Chief," said the driver. "Point-five miles per hour."

"I want you to get on the loudspeaker," said Daniels. "Make an announcement that the train will be delayed just a few minutes due to mechanical trouble. Apologize (apologise) for the delay. Use the same words you always do for the announcement. We don't want to alarm the passengers."

There was silence as the driver made the announcement.

"Did you by any chance see three men with backpacks get on at Fulton Street?" Chief Daniels asked the driver.

"I did, Chief," said the driver. "I checked my mirror before I closed the doors. They were almost the only people who got on. In fact, I think they are in the second car behind me." The task force room burst into action. The *officers* were shouting into their phones.

"The driver says that three men with backpacks got on together at Fulton Street! They are at the front of the train, probably in the second car from the front!"

Übung 85: Markieren Sie die richtige Antwort!

1. Will you go to the theatre on Saturday?
a) ☐ Not probably.
b) ☐ Probably not.

2. Do you think it will rain tomorrow?
a) ☐ Probably.
b) ☐ Likely.

3. How likely is it that he will come?
a) ☐ Some likely.
b) ☐ Very likely.

4. Would you open this jar for me?
a) ☐ Not likely.
b) ☐ Certainly.

5. Will you finish before noon?
a) ☐ Perhaps.
b) ☐ Most perhaps.

6. Are they in the last car?
a) ☐ Not possibly.
b) ☐ Probably not.

In every corner of the room, men and women were issuing orders into their phones.
"Get those people off the *subway* platform! Now! Now!"
"I want every uniformed *officer* you've got!"
"This is not a drill! Get those people off the platform!"

"Now! Now!"

As quickly as they could, the *officers* made plans to use whatever personnel were closest to Court Street.

Chief Ruiz was the NYPD chief closest to the Court Street station in Brooklyn. He was on a regular phone line with Chief Daniels. Daniels still held his mobile phone to his other ear, to maintain contact with the driver of the train.

"I've got twenty armed men with bulletproof shields and automatic weapons going down the stairway at Court Street Station," reported Ruiz. "They will be behind the stairway at the front of the train when it pulls in."

"I want another ten plainclothes *officers* standing all along the platform," said Chief Daniels. "I don't want the robbers wondering why there is no one in sight."

"Roger," said Chief Ruiz. Chief Daniels heard him yelling to his lieutenants.

"Make sure some of those armed men are spread out along the length of the platform," said Daniels into the phone, "just in case the robbers are located in a different car."

"Right," said Ruiz.

Agent O'Leary gestured for Chief Daniels' attention. "Put Ruiz on the speaker phone, so we can all hear him."

O'Leary, too, was on a mobile phone. "They're sending down ten plainclothes *officers* from the MTA," reported O'Leary. "That's all they've got. The undercover *officers* will clear any passengers out of the station and onto the street as quickly as they can. The uniformed *officers* will take up positions at the head of each stairway. Backup is on the way from the NYPD. Those guys will secure the exits and the perimeter, and stand by on the mezzanine level just in case anything goes wrong downstairs."

"That's great, O'Leary," said Chief Daniels.

Looey spoke up. "Emergency Services says they have a helicopter in the area. It will be over Court Street in two minutes. A second helicopter just lifted off from Floyd Bennett Field."
Inspector Hudson watched silently. The crucial information he provided had set off a storm of activity. The best way he could help was to stand by. Hudson remembered the words of the poet John Milton: "They also serve who only stand and wait."

ÜBUNG 86 !

Übung 86: Übersetzen Sie ins Deutsche!

1. mezzanine ____________________
2. perimeter ____________________
3. to secure ____________________
4. undercover agent ____________________
5. plainclothes *officer* ____________________
6. crucial ____________________
7. backup ____________________
8. drill ____________________

"Where exactly is that train?" shouted O'Leary. "How many minutes have we got?"
O'Leary turned to Hudson and said, half to himself. "I want to know exactly where those guys are. I want as many passengers as possible out of our way. I can't risk killing civilians to get at three bank robbers. And I can't have them taking innocent people hostage."

"How many minutes?" called Inspector Hudson.

Ozbek was the quickest with a calculator.

"At this speed, sir, about … eight."

O'Leary took the telephone receiver out of Chief Daniels' hand. "How are you doing, Ruiz?"

"My people are on the platform, moving all passengers off the platform and up the stairs," reported Chief Ruiz, from Brooklyn. "The twenty men in riot gear, with bulletproof shields, are on their way."

"They had better be running, Ruiz."

"You can bet on it, O'Leary."

"I want them behind the stairs where the people on the train cannot see them as it pulls in."

"I read you, O'Leary. They have their instructions. They never put on their gear so fast in their lives. I'm going after them right now. I'm going to leave this phone line open."

Agent O'Leary let out a long breath.

Inspector Hudson was standing silently next to Agent O'Leary.

O'Leary said, "We've *practiced* (practised) for emergencies, Hudson. Fires, floods, bombs, biological agents, chemical warfare. Any kind of emergency. We *practice* and *practice.* But you never know …"

"The cooperation among the agencies is most impressive," said Hudson.

Agent O'Leary finally smiled.

"You know, Hudson – that's the hardest trick of all. The people on the forces are not the problem. It's the chiefs."

O'Leary smiled again.

"I'm no exception," he admitted. "But what's the alternative? Right now, for example, I'd love to be in charge down there, but Ruiz is on the spot, and I'm not. He has to do whatever he thinks is best."

"Sometimes," said Hudson, "the hardest thing is to wait."

Übung 87: Ordnen Sie richtig zu!

a) traffic light
b) desk sergeant
c) transit police
d) photocopier
e) token booth
f) mezzanine
g) crosstown street
h) cashpoint machine
i) tracks
j) remote control
k) fax machine
l) traffic

1. in the subway

2. at the task force headquarters

3. around the city

"We're down! We're down!" shouted Ruiz over the speaker phone. "I'm on the platform with a raincoat over my uniform. We're all in position."

The people in Manhattan heard Ruiz shout out his last orders to the people on the platform.

"The train is pulling in!" shouted Ruiz. "I see the light!"

The speaker phone was on full volume at the task force headquarters in Manhattan. Everyone heard the sound of a *subway* train slowly pulling into the station. The screech of the brakes filled the room.

"Driver, do not open the doors on your train," said Chief Daniels into his mobile. "Do not open the doors."

"There are three men with backpacks standing in the front of the second car," reported Ruiz. "They are alone in the car. I am just going to leave this phone line open, Daniels. It's time to go."
There was a moment's pause.

Übung 88: Unterstreichen Sie die sieben Verben in Imperativform!

ÜBUNG 88 !

"Hold it steady, driver," said Daniels into the mobile. "Wait until I tell you to open the doors."
"Draw your weapons!" shouted Ruiz. "Now! Go!"
Twenty uniformed *officers* in full riot gear stepped out from behind the stairs. They quickly formed a semi-circle around the train door nearest the three robbers.
"Do not open your doors, driver," repeated Daniels.
"This is the police!" shouted Ruiz. "You are surrounded! Put up your hands!"
The three men stared, expressionless, at the army that waited for them on the platform. Ten men behind bulletproof shields stood with their weapons drawn right outside the train door. Another ten *officers* with shields had formed a bulletproof wall between the robbers' car and the rest of the train. It was over.
"Put up your hands!"

Without looking at one another, the robbers slowly raised their hands.
"Higher!" shouted Ruiz. "Driver, open your doors!"
"Open your doors, driver," said Chief Daniels, calmly, into the mobile phone.
Over the speaker phone, they heard the sound of the train doors opening, and the sound of running feet. They heard police *officers*

urging the passengers: “This way! This way! Quickly, this is an emergency! Let us help you, sir. We’ll get that chair later.”
The rest was strangely silent.
“Keep your hands in the air,” said Chief Ruiz, in a steadier voice. He was no longer shouting, and seemed to be closer to the action.
“They’re disarming the robbers,” said O’Leary, to no one in particular.
“Keep your hands in the air,” repeated Ruiz. There was a pause and he spoke again.
“I am Chief Ruiz of the New York Police Department. Are you *Mr*. Masterson?”
The voice of an Englishman was heard, loud and clear, in reply.
“How do you do?”

! ÜBUNG 89

Übung 89: Tragen Sie ***a, an*** *oder* ***the*** *ein oder lassen Sie das Feld leer!*

The task force headquarters was hung with 1. ______ red, white and blue banners to celebrate 2. ______ capture of Michael Masterson and his two partners in 3. ______ crime. On the wall hung 4. ______ enormous poster of 5. ______ New York City *Subway* System. Right next to it hung 6. ______ poster of 7. ______ London Underground that Sergeant Jones had printed out from 8. ______ internet.

Inspector James Hudson walked in the door, fresh from his trip to Brooklyn to verify the identity of Michael Masterson.

A cheer went up. “Inspector Hudson!” the partygoers cried. “Hear, hear!”
They pulled him to the front of the crowd and made him give a speech.

Übung 90: Setzen Sie die passenden Wörter aus der folgenden Liste in die Lücken ein!
(thwarted, vigilant, convicted, notorious, enforcement, petty)

“We are here to celebrate the cooperation between the law 1. ________________ agencies of the United States and the United Kingdom,” announced Inspector Hudson. “Together, we have brought to justice a 2. ________________ criminal. As you know, Scotland Yard was searching for Michael Masterson, a 3. ________________ felon. You were looking for him, too – ”
“Though we didn’t know it!” yelled Sergeant Ozbek.
“The Skyline Syndicate has been 4. ________________,” continued Inspector Hudson. “Without a powerful leader, they will fade back into 5. ________________ crime. We will remain ever 6. ________________, on both sides of the Atlantic, to prevent their rising to power again.”

A cheer went up.
“Speaking of the skyline,” said Inspector Hudson, “I’d like to add

that I will never forget the taxi ride from the airport into the city. The skyline of Manhattan rising above New York Harbor is a spectacular sight! No wonder the syndicate wanted the skyline for its name!"

Inspector Hudson smiled at his new friends.

"But that led to our mistake. We looked for the syndicate in Manhattan. But the most beautiful view of the skyline can only be seen from Brooklyn!"

"And that's where we found the Skyline Syndicate!" shouted everyone.

"I am very grateful for the opportunity I had to get to know New York and so many fine police *officers*. I shall miss you all very much."

"And we'll miss you, Inspector!" they all cried.

"We'll never forget you, sir," added Lieutenant Louise LaCapra.

O'Leary stepped forward and announced, "In the excitement of the last days, there is something very important that we forgot to do."

Everyone looked puzzled.

"We never officially deputized (deputised) Inspector Hudson."

The whole room laughed.

O'Leary turned to Hudson. "Please raise your right hand."

Eugene O'Leary administered the oath of office, and James Hudson was officially sworn in.

"You're one of us now," cried the New Yorkers. "*Take care* (Look after yourself)!"

Abschlusstest

Übung 1: Setzen Sie die richtige Verbform ein!

1. Miss Paddington (be) ________ concerned that her employer not get lost.
2. Sir Reginald (want) ____________ Hudson to go on vacation before this, but Hudson (not want) ____________ to go.
3. Agent O'Leary (ring up) _______________ the train driver.
4. Assistant Chief Constable Stanley normally (reside) _________ ____________ in Liverpool, but this month he (work) _________ ____________ in New York.
5. Carolyn LaCapra (not be) ______________________ usually assigned to the same department as her sister.
6. Looey (take) _________________ Hudson to Times Square, but she was busy.

Übung 2: Setzen Sie die folgenden Sätze in die direkte Rede! Achten Sie auf die Zeitform!

1. Miss Paddington said that she would like to see New York.

____

2. Sergeant Jones said that there was no inspector.

____

3. Agent O'Leary said that it was getting late.

____

4. The woman said that her son was innocent and never committed a crime.

____

5. Assistant Chief Constable Stanley said that he worked in Liverpool when he was called to New York.

____

____

6. Looey said that Carolyn was her sister.

____

Übung 3: Sie rufen jemanden an. Ihr Gesprächspartner meldet sich. Was sagen Sie als nächstes? Kreuzen Sie die richtige Aussage an!

1. Hello. My name is Susan Gifford.
a) ☐ I am a teacher at the Tottenham Institute.
b) ☐ You meant to call me.

2. Hello. My name is Angela Reskin.
a) ☐ Do you know why I'm calling?
b) ☐ I read in the newspaper that you are looking to hire a secretary.

3. Good morning. My name is Mr Rogers.

a) ☐ I would like to register for the course in English conversation.

b) ☐ I cannot get through to you on the phone.

Übung 4: Sind die Wörter britisch oder amerikanisch?

1. elevator ______________________
2. cellphone ______________________
3. kerb ______________________
4. lorry ______________________
5. tuxedo ______________________
6. faucet ______________________
7. lorry ______________________
8. queue ______________________

Übung 5: Ordnen Sie den Dialog!

1. "What did you learn?"
2. "Yes, sir. I learned a lot about police work in a big city."
3. "It is important to know the city inside and out."
4. "Did you enjoy your trip to New York, Hudson?"
5. "Yes, sir. London is my home."
6. "And are you glad to be back?"

Lösung: _ _ _ _ _ _

Übung 6: Füllen Sie das Kreuzworträtsel aus! Das Lösungswort ist der Name eines berühmten Wolkenkratzers in der Nähe von Grand Central Station.

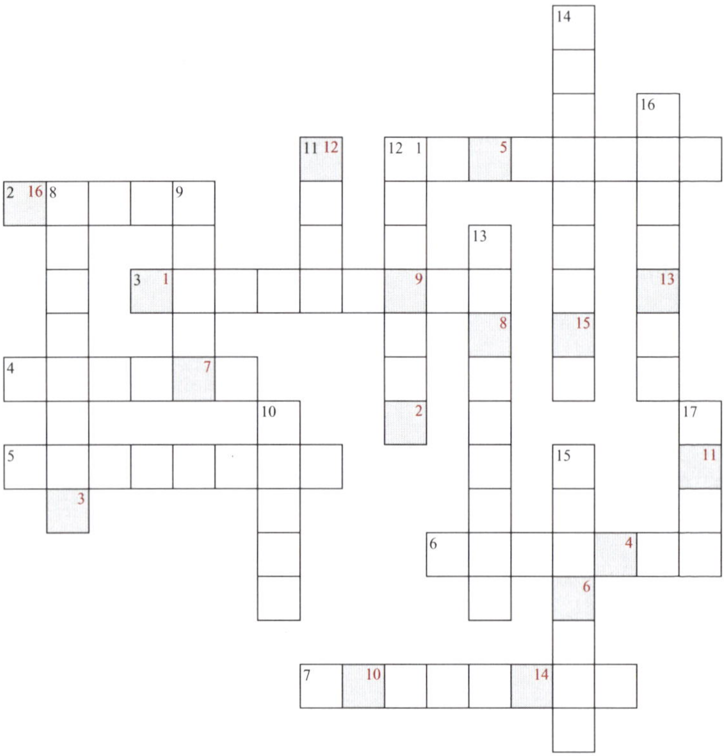

Horizontal: 1. Amerikanisch für "toilet", 2. Britisch für *men's room,* 3. Britisch für *police officer*, 4. Amerikanisch für "tap", 5. Britisch für *highway*, 6. Britisch für ((analyze)), 7. Britisch für *boss*
Vertikal: 8. Amerikanisch für "lift", 9. Britisch für ((fourteen pounds)), 10. Amerikanisch für "trousers", 11. Britisch für *elevator*, 12. Britisch für *garbage*, 13. Britisch für *airplane*, 14. Amerikanisch für "flat", 15. Amerikanisch für ((porter)), 16. Britisch für *vacation*, 17. Amerikanisch für "queue"

Lösungswort: _ _ _ _ _ _ _ _   _ _ _ _ _ _ _ _

Übung 7: Finden Sie das richtige Lösungswort heraus!

1. Person who takes the subway to work: _ _ _ _ _ ☐ _ _
2. Means of public transportation: _ ☐ _ _ _
3. Grand Central is a large: _ _ ☐ _ _ _ ☐
4. Painted on the ceiling in Grand Central: ☐ _ _ _ _
5. Grand Central is in this section of Manhattan: _ ☐ _ _ _ _ _
6. The clock tells the: ☐ _ _ _

Lösung: _ _ _ _ _ _ _

Übung 8: Erinnern Sie sich an die Situationen im Buch? Finden Sie heraus, welche der Aussagen im geschilderten Zusammenhang zutrifft!

1. Hudson asks Sir Reginald: “Why does a crime committed in New York concern Scotland Yard?” Sir Reginald replies:
   a) ☐ “The Skyline Syndicate is a very important organization.”
   b) ☐ “The crime may cross national boundaries.”
   c) ☐ “The FBI has specifically requested you, Hudson.”

2. Hudson says to Miss Paddington: “I have been assigned to work with the FBI in New York!” Miss Paddington replies:
   a) ☐ “But they deal with the most violent crimes, sir! Aren’t you worried?”
   b) ☐ “I hear the New York police constables are armed, sir. Shouldn’t you carry a weapon?”

c) ☐ "It would be wise not to travel on the Underground *(ride the subway)* until you learn how to behave in the city."

3. You ask a cab driver: "Do you think it's safe to ride the *subway*?" He replies:
   a) ☐ "Oh yes, my children take the *subway* to school every day."
   b) ☐ "The *subway* is convenient, but it doesn't make enough stops in Manhattan."
   c) ☐ "Many people think public transportation has become too expensive."

4. You ask the *desk clerk* at the Ivy Club: "Can you direct me to the nearest *ATM machine*?" She replies:
   a) ☐ "I would be happy to give you up to two hundred dollars, if you'll sign right here."
   b) ☐ "There's a bank on the next corner. Just turn right once you leave the Club."
   c) ☐ "Many banks have discontinued this service, after the recent robberies."

5. You are introduced to Agent O'Leary, and you ask: "How are things going at *task force headquarters*?" Agent O'Leary replies:
   a) ☐ "For many reasons, the incidence of violent crime in New York has been steadily decreasing."
   b) ☐ "We are trying to narrow down the possible escape routes, so that we can get a better idea where to look for the criminals."
   c) ☐ "Our budget has been cut, because the money was needed to increase security at Grand Central Station."

6. Assistant Chief Constable Stanley explains to you that he has been cross-deputized (cross-deputised) in New York. You ask:

a) ☐ "Are you in New York as part of a general exchange program, or are you only authorized (authorised) to work on a particular crime?
b) ☐ "Does that mean you have been permanently transferred to New Jersey?"
c) ☐ "But isn't it illegal to serve in another country?"

7. You ask Patrol Officer LaCapra: "Can I take the R train from Times Square to Union Square?" She replies:
a) ☐ "Yes, but it will take you to Brooklyn first."
b) ☐ "Yes, but it would be faster to take the N train, because it is an express."
c) ☐ "No, because you must have exact change for the fare."

8. Chief Daniels asks Chief Ruiz: "Are all the passengers off the subway platform?"
a) ☐ "Yes! We must be able to see the train as it comes in!"
b) ☐ "Yes! I cannot allow the robbers to take innocent people hostage!"
c) ☐ "No! It is more important to secure every exit of the station!"

Übung 9: Übersetzen Sie die folgenden Sätze ins Englische!

1. Sir Reginald schickte Inspector Hudson nach New York, um einen Bankraub aufzuklären.

2. Das Taxi fuhr am Ufer entlang und Inspector Hudson sah die Skyline von New York.

3. Lieutenant Louise LaCapra möchte nicht unhöflich sein, aber sie ist oft etwas zu direkt.

4. Meinen Sie, wir werden einen Hubschrauber schicken müssen?

5. Wird die Polizei in Brooklyn bereit sein, bevor der Zug in der Station eintrifft?

6. Wenn Chief Daniels den Zugführer angewiesen hätte, den Zug anzuhalten, hätte dieser ihn angehalten.

7. Die Polizei hätte die Räuber früher gefasst, doch sie hat am falschen Ort gesucht.

____

____

8. Hätten Sie den zweiten Raubüberfall verhindern können, wenn sie gewusst hätten, dass der Räuber Michael Masterson war?

____

____

Übung 10: Setzen Sie, wenn nötig, die richtige Präposition ein!

1. Patel lives _______ Brooklyn.
2. She took the train _______ New Jersey.
3. The train leaves _______ Grand Central.
4. The first stop is _______ Times Square.
5. We must look _______ clues!
6. That tunnel goes _______ the river to Brooklyn.
7. The detective asked _______ the suspect's previous record.
8. Can you see any reason _______ the suspect's behaviour?
9. Two cops started masking _______ the area with yellow and black crime scene tape.
10. The FBI could rule _______ a car.

Lösungen

Übung 1: 1. b 2. a 3. b 4. b 5. a 6. b 7. b

Übung 2: 1. Has Inspector Hudson been to New York? 2. Are the Rockettes chorus girls? 3. Are they dancers in New York? 4. Is Inspector Hudson shocked? 5. Is Inspector Hudson interested in chorus girls? 6. Will he spend his day off at the British Museum? 7. Does Sir Reginald think he is a queer bird?

Übung 3: 1. smell 2. bacon 3. long 4. time 5. down 6. eggs 7. such 8. work

Übung 4: 1. bitter orange 2. soft-boiled 3. tea 4. rashers 5. butter Lösung: toast

Übung 5: 1. vacation 2. bacon 3. I'm not interested. 4. Get some rest! 5. expensive 6. boss

Übung 6: 1. teakettle 2. work 3. bird 4. badge 5. direction 6. habit 7. book

Übung 7: 1. a 2. b 3. b 4. b

Übung 8: Unterstrichen: 1. old 2. beautiful 3. modest 4. conservative 5. British 6. careful 7. glad 8. surprised 9. enjoys 10. proud

Übung 9: 1. a 2. b 3. a 4. b 5. b 6. a 7. b

Übung 10: 1. replied 2. robbed 3. million 4. shot 5. asking 6. office 7. instantly 8. bag 9. airport

Übung 11: Unterstrichen: 1. good 2. worried 3. loudly 4. immediately 5. straightaway 6. planned 7. exactly 8. early

Übung 12: Durchgestrichen: 1. My mother told me so. 2. He gave them the bill. 3. Dinner is getting cold! 4. You have told me this before. 5. Why should I believe you? 6. I offered him help. 7. He bought a new car.

Übung 13: 1. major 2. international 3. worldwide 4. young 5. odd 6. freelance 7. individual 8. huge 9. international 10. miserable 11. nylon 12. distorted

Übung 14: 1. ... noted similarities. 2. ... wore nylon stockings. 3. ... says it is not original. 4. ... made tea and toast. 5. ... got a phone call. 6. ... will cooperate with the FBI. 7. ... may be going international.

Übung 15: 1. richtig 2. Let's videotape the party! 3. richtig 4. richtig 5. richtig 6. richtig 7. Did you watch a video last night? 8. richtig 9. Let's rent some videos!

Übung 16: 1. I must admit that 2. It seems to me that 3. It's possible 4. Might it be 5. Let me 6. It's not my cup of tea 7. Perhaps I misunderstood 8. Could we possibly 9. May I

Übung 17: 4, 2, 5, 7, 1, 3, 8, 6

Übung 18: 1. I'll call you up tomorrow! 2. I left it in my apartment! 3. Right away, sir! 4. Take her to the emergency room! 5. Really? 6. Take a look! 7. That's right!

Übung 19: Unterstrichen: 1. of 2. with 3. by 4. with 5. in 6. of

Übung 20: 1. mean, baseball bat, overweight, attempted murder 2. robber, not clever, gun, liquor store

Übung 21: 1. a 2. a 3. b 4. a 5. a 6. a 7. b

Übung 22: 1. mobile 2. number plate 3. holiday 4. phone box 5. stone 6. aeroplane

Übung 23: 1. a 2. b 3. a 4. b 5. b 6. a 7. a

Übung 24: 1. breakdown lane 2. gas 3. highway 4. trunk 5. gas station 6. truck 7. curb 8. line 9. subway

Übung 25: 1. Londoners 2. Englishmen and Englishwomen 3. New Yorkers 4. Americans 5. Indians 6. Italians 7. Brooklynites 8. Manhattanites 9. New Jerseyans 10. Liverpudlians

Übung 26: 1. Every 2. narrow 3. high 4. built 5. longest 6. go 7. driver 8. water 9. there 10. laughed

Übung 27: 1. protection money 2. tug boat 3. suspension bridge 4. police constable 5. ocean liner 6. cab driver 7. real life 8. petrol station 9. mobile phone 10. breakdown lane 11. airline terminal 12. phone booth

Übung 28: 1. seriously 2. aid 3. perpetrators 4. sympathy 5. wounds 6. call 7. regret 8. bring to justice 9. off-duty 10. extend

Übung 29: 1. asked Inspector Hudson 2. laughed 3. said the cabbie 4. smiled Inspector Hudson 5. agreed the cabbie 6. nodded 7. exclaimed

Übung 30: 3, 2, 5, 6, 4, 1, 8, 7, 9

Übung 31: Unterstrichen: 1. asked 2. nodded 3. asked 4. said 5. asked 6. exclaimed 7. agreed

Übung 32: 1. turned 2. pulled 3. impressed 4. Wait 5. tell 6. drove 7. pressed 8. printed 9. kidding

Übung 33: 1. amerikanisch 2. beides 3. britisch 4. amerikanisch 5. amerikanisch 6. britisch

Übung 34: 1. That is 2. It is 3. everyone is 4. You would 5. I would 6. It is

Übung 35: 1. spoke – talked 2. high – tall 3. examined – inspected 4. directly – non-stop 5. training – education 6. tired – sleepy 7. corridor – hallway 8. getaway – escape 9. footpath – sidewalk

Übung 36: 1. Thank you! 2. Splendid, thank you! 3. My name is Inspector Hudson. 4. My friends call me James. 5. Yes, this is my first trip to the United States. 6. No, I have never been to New York before.

Übung 37: 1. Inspector Hudson 2. Fat Frankie 3. Salvatore del Monaco 4. Agent O'Leary 5. *Officer* Mahoney 6. Skyline Syndicate 7. Inspector Hudson

Übung 38: 1. It's a pleasure to meet you, Miss Perkins. 2. Stand up. 3. The pleasure is mine. 4. Stand up. 5. Good evening, Mr Ambassador. 6. "I don't think so."

Übung 39: 1. was 2. read 3. proved 4. had fixed 5. recovered 6. stopped 7. smiled

Übung 40: 1. blue eyes 2. curly hair 3. slim build 4. fair complexion 5. female gender 6. 5 feet 8 inches

Übung 41: 1. Dürfte ich bitte Ihre Kreditkarte sehen? 2. Wo ist der nächste Geldautomat, bitte? 3. Ich habe meine PIN Nummer vergessen! 4. Geben Sie jetzt Ihre Kontonummer ein. 5. Wählen Sie die zwei für Deutsch. 6. Geben Sie jetzt Ihr Kennwort ein. 7. Bitte entnehmen Sie Ihre Karte.

Übung 42: 1. Would you care for a biscuit? 2. I'd like a cup of coffee. 3. I would prefer a cup of tea. 4. Do you have chocolate cake today? 5. I'd like six jelly doughnuts. 6. May I have a glass of water? 7. Do you (still) serve warm food?

Übung 43: 1. britisch 2. amerikanisch 3. britisch 4. britisch 5. beides 6. amerikanisch 7. britisch

Übung 44: 1. politely 2. slightly 3. quietly 4. pointedly 5. dramatically 6. casually

Übung 45: 1. in 2. – 3. on 4. – 5. in 6. on 7. on 8. through to 9. at

Übung 46: 1. Farewell 2. See you in the morning. 3. I had a lovely evening. 4. Good bye. 5. Sleep tight. 6. Good night.

Übung 47: 1. Half an hour later 2. morning 3. morning 4. early 5. lag 6. morning

Übung 48: 1. bacon 2. eggs 3. English muffins 4. porridge 5. porridge 6. tofu 7. tofu 8. eggs 9. rashers 10. toast 11. orange marmalade

Übung 49: 1. closed 2. quite 3. night 4. single 5. people 6. around 7. nobody 8. middle

Übung 50: 1. five forty 2. half a million 3. 1:00 4. 6 p.m. 5. 2:15 6. 7:30 7. 8:15

Übung 51: 1. britisch: Wirf es weg! 2. britisch: die Teile in den Müll werfen 3. amerikanisch: den Müll rausbringen 4. britisch: Müllmann 5. britisch: Müllbeutel 6. amerikanisch: Müllabfuhr

Übung 52: 1. straggled 2. party 3. worse 4. businessmen 5. leftover 6. stared 7. joined 8. unfortunate

Übung 53: 1. Please remain calm. 2. We are closed. 3. First door to the right. 4. There's another one at six. 5. That way! 6. I'll get out my dinner jacket.

Übung 54: 1. c 2. a 3. c 4. b 5. c

Übung 55: 1. Verrazano – New York Harbour 2. Henry Hudson – Hudson River 3. Inspector Hudson – Grand Central Station 4. Arjun Patel – Brooklyn 5. Narragansett Tribe – Newport Bay 6. the King of France – nowhere

Übung 56: 1. richtig 2. falsch 3. richtig 4. richtig 5. richtig 6. richtig 7. richtig 8. richtig 9. richtig 10. richtig 11. falsch

Übung 57: 1. on 2. in 3. of 4. into 5. In 6. up

Übung 58: 1. tyre 2. favourite 3. travelled 4. honour 5. savour 6. labour 7. licence 8. centre

Übung 59: 1. Manhattan 2. uptown, midtown and downtown 3. midtown 4. west 5. train number 7 and the shuttle 6. uptown and downtown

Übung 60: 1. beides 2. beides 3. britisch 4. beides 5. beides 6. beides 7. britisch

Übung 61: 1. Can't you 2. They're 3. one's 4. That's 5. Let's 6. there's 7. We'll

Übung 62: 1. he wondered. 2. he conceded. 3. she urged. 4. she commanded. 5. she mused. 6. he yelled. 7. she hissed.

Übung 63: 7, 3, 5, 1, 4, 2, 8, 6

Übung 64: struggling, anything, walking, floating, listening, recording (The "-ing" in "anything" is part of".)

Übung 65: 1. Chief Stanley called to them from across the room. 2. She is Fat Frankie's wife. 3. Hudson and Looey stared at the screen. 4. She's also got a lot of money. 5. He looked very pleased with himself 6. Agent O'Leary appeared in the doorway.

Übung 66: 1. let's eat lunch! 2. Frankie will kill him. 3. I would have said hello. 4. please call. 5. 'll go, too. 6. he's wrong 7. you'll get to Times Square.

Übung 67: 1. richtig 2. richtig 3. wraps and three cokes® 4. richtig 5. richtig 6. salad 7. with rice

Übung 68: 1. riper, ripest 2. bigger, biggest 3. worse, worst 4. older, oldest 5. smaller, smallest 6. more extreme, most extreme 7. further/farther, furthest/farthest 8. prettier, prettiest

Übung 69: 1. a 2. a 3. b 4. a 5. a

Übung 70: 1. Chinese 2. Italian 3. Irish 4. African-American 5. Turkish 6. Indian

Übung 71: 3, 5, 6, 1, 4, 2

Übung 72: 1. theater 2. criticize 3. realize 4. analyze 5. deputize 6. practice 7. water

Übung 73: 1. downtown 2. west, to Times Square 3. Times Square

Übung 74: 1. traveling 2. fulfill 3. skillful 4. jewelry 5. draft 6. plow

Übung 75: 1. near Grand Central Station. 2. downtown. 3. to Times Square. 4. change trains. 5. at Union Square. 6. different directions. 7. together.

Übung 76: 1. near 2. into/out of 3. as far as 4. edge 5. up 6. bottom

Übung 77: 1. slow motion 2. rose up 3. deadly force 4. bending deeply 5. struck hard 6. same time

Übung 78: 1 falsch 2. falsch 3. richtig 4. falsch 5. falsch 6. falsch

Übung 79: 1. Fine, thank you. 2. She is very well, thank you. 3. He recommended bed rest. 4. I was, but I'm better now. 5. My temperature is 100.2.

Übung 80: 1. post 2. watched 3. played 4. caught 5. videotaped 6. rent

Übung 81: 1. thrilled 2. crushed 3. ecstatic 4. furious 5. starved 6. depressed

Übung 82: 1. pace 2. breezy 3. crocodiles 4. Piccadilly Circus 5. mid-town 6. stable

Übung 83: 1. Brooklyn 2. train 3. Court Street 4. telephone 5. line 6. *up* 7. O'Leary's

Übung 84: 1. Looey said: "The trip takes seven minutes." 2. Patel said to Hudson: "I took the man to Brooklyn." 3. The driver asked: "What's wrong?" 4. Looey said: "We might have enough time." 5. Chief Daniels told the driver: "Do not stop the train." 6. Looey said: "I hope he isn't sleeping." 7. Patel said: "On the morning of the robbery, before the news was out, I picked up a guy at Union Square."

Übung 85: 1. b 2. a 3. b 4. b 5. a 6. b

Übung 86: 1. Zwischen-/Halbgeschoss, Mezzanin 2. Peripherie 3. sichern 4. Geheimagent 5. Polizist in Zivil 6. kritisch 7. Unterstützung 8. Übung

Übung 87: 1. c, e, f, i 2. b, d, j ,k 3. a, g, h, l

Übung 88: 1. Hold 2. Wait 3. Draw 4. Go 5. Do not open 6. Put up 7. Put up

Übung 89: 1. – 2. the 3. – 4. an 5. the 6. a 7. the 8. the

Übung 90: 1. enforcement 2. notorious 3. convicted 4. thwarted 5. petty 6. vigilant

Lösungen Abschlusstest

Übung 1: 1. was 2. wanted, did not want 3. rang up 4. resides, is working 5. is not 6. would have taken

Übung 2: 1. Miss Paddington said: "I would like to see New York." 2. Sergeant Jones said: "There is no inspector." 3. Agent O'Leary said: "It is getting late." 4. The woman said: "My son is innocent and has never committed a crime." 5. Assistant Chief Constable

Stanley said: "I was working in Liverpool when I was called to New York." 6. Looey said: "Carolyn is my sister."

Übung 3: 1 a. 2. b 3. a

Übung 4: 1. amerikanisch 2. amerikanisch 3. britisch 4. britisch 5. amerikanisch 6. amerikanisch 7. britisch 8. britisch

Übung 5: 4, 2, 1, 3, 6, 5

Übung 6:
Horizontal: 1. restroom 2. *gents* 3. constable 4. *faucet* 5. motorway 6. analyse 7. superior
Vertikal: 8. *elevator* 9. stone 10. *pants* 11. lift 12. rubbish 13. aeroplane 14. *apartment* 15. *bellhop* 16. holiday 17. *line*
Lösungswort: Chrysler building

Übung 7: 1. commuter 2. train 3. station 4. stars 5. midtown 6. time
Lösung: transit

Übung 8: 1. b 2. c 3. a 4. b 5. b 6. a 7. b 8. b

Übung 9: 1. Sir Reginald sent Inspector Hudson to New York to solve a bank robbery. 2. The taxi drove along the shore and Inspector Hudson saw the skyline of New York. 3. Lieutenant Louise LaCapra does not mean to be impolite, but she is often a bit too direct. 4. Do you think we will have to send a helicopter? 5. Will the police in Brooklyn be ready before the train arrives in the station? 6. If Chief Daniels had told the driver to stop the train, he would have stopped it. 7. The police would have caught the robbers sooner, but they were looking in the wrong place. 8. Could they have prevented the second robbery, if they had known that the robber was Michael Masterson?

Übung 10: 1. in 2. to 3. from 4. – 5. for 6. under 7. about 8. for 9. off 10. out